Cognitive Behavior Therapy of DSM-IV Personality Disorders

Cognitive Behavior Therapy of DSM-IV Personality Disorders

Highly Effective Interventions for the Most Common Personality Disorders

Len Sperry, M.D., Ph.D.

BRUNNER/MAZEL
Taylor & Francis Group

USA	Publishing Office	Brunner/Mazel A member of the Taylor & Francis Group 325 Chestnut Street, Suite 800 Philadelphia, PA 19106 Tel: (215) 625-8900 Fax: (215) 625-2940
	Distribution Center	Brunner/Mazel A member of the Taylor & Francis Group 7625 Empire Drive Florence, KY 41042 Tel: (800) 634-7064 Fax: (800) 248-4724
UK		Brunner/Mazel A member of the Taylor & Francis Group 11 New Fetter Lane London EC4P 4EE Tel: +44 (0) 171 583 9855 Fax: +44 (0) 171 842 2298

COGNITIVE BEHAVIOR THERAPY OF DSM-IV PERSONALITY DISORDERS: Highly Effective Interventions for the Most Common Personality Disorders

5   6   7   8   9   0

Printed by Edwards Brothers, Ann Arbor, MI, 1999.
Cover design by Carolyn O'Brien

A CIP catalog record for this book is available from the British Library.

The paper in this publication meets the requirements of the ANSI Standard Z39.48-1984 (Permanence of Paper).

Library of Congress Cataloging-in-Publication Data

Sperry, Len.
    Cognitive behavior therapy of DSM-IV personality disorders : highly effective interventions for the most common personality disorders / Len Sperry.
    Includes index.
    ISBN 0-87630-900-7 (case : alk. paper)
    1. Personality disorders—Treatment.   2. Cognitive therapy.   I. Title.
RC554.S67   1999
616.85'8—dc21
                                                            98–54187
                                                               CIP

ISBN: 0-87630-900-7

CONTENTS

FOREWARD

We have all had the experience of taking a mid-morning coffee break and meeting a colleague in the coffee room only to find them staring into their cup. When we ask what they are experiencing they would respond, "I just saw three patients with severe depression in a row. I really feel down and need this coffee to pick me up." Or we might see a colleague in the coffee room in a state of high arousal and question them about their agitation. They might respond, "I just saw three patients with severe panic disorder in a row, and need the coffee to calm me down." Or we might take a mid-morning break and on our way to the coffee room we find a colleague wandering aimlessly through the corridors on their way to get coffee. We take them by the arm and guide them to the coffee room because we know that they have just seen three patients with severe personality disorder.

Given the long-term nature of patients with severe personality disorders, their general avoidance of psychotherapy, their frequent referral through family pressure or legal remand, and their seeming reluctance or inability to change, they are often the most difficult patients in a clinician's caseload. They generally require more work within a session, a longer time for therapy, and more therapist energy than do virtually any other patients. All of this expenditure occurs without the same rate of change and satisfaction as is gained with other patients.

These individuals typically come for therapy with presenting issues other than personality problems, most often with more typical Axis I complaints of depression and anxiety. The reported problems may be separate and apart from the Axis II patterns or derived and fueled by the Axis II personality disorder. For the combination of Axis I and Axis II diagnoses, the course of treatment is far more complicated than for the typical non-Axis II patient with the same presenting Axis I complaints. The duration of treatment, frequency of treatment sessions, goals and expectations for both therapist and patient, and the available techniques and strategies need to be altered in the treatment of patients who are diagnosed with personality disorders.

The personality disordered patient will often see the difficulties that they encounter in dealing with other people or tasks as outside of them and independent of their behavior. Their behavior is generally ego-syntonic. Their behavior somehow makes sense to them and serves as part of their long-standing survival and coping strategies. Their style of behaving and responding seems normal and reasonable to them and they generally see the problems that they encounter in life as a product of other people's inappropriate behavior or ill-will.

A patient with a personality disorder may have little idea about how they got to be the way they are, how they contribute to their life problems, or how to change. They are often referred by family members or friends who recognize a dysfunctional pattern or who have reached their personal limit in attempting to cope with this individual. Still other patients are referred by the judicial system. This latter group are often given a choice; for example, to go to prison or go to therapy. Other personality disordered patients are very much aware of the self-defeating nature of their personality problems (e.g., overdependence, inhibition, excessive avoidance) but are at a real loss as to how to change these patterns. Still other patients may have the motivation to change but do not have the skills to change.

The therapy of patients with various disorders of character or personality have been discussed in the clinical literature since the beginning of the recorded history of psychotherapy. The general literature on the psychotherapeutic treatment of personality disorders has emerged more recently and is growing quickly. The main theoretical orientation in the psychotherapeutic literature has been psychoanalytic. More recently, cognitive-behavioral therapists have offered a structured, active, and directive treatment approach and have advocated using a wide range of cognitive and behavioral techniques depending on the level of severity of the dysfunction. This is the first book I know of that convincingly emphasizes the clinical importance and relevance of the temperament dimension in the treatment of personality disorders.

Whereas some personality disorders are diagnosed rather early in treatment, a clinician may not be aware initially of the characterological nature, chronicity, and severity of the patient's personality problems. Early diagnosis is essential to appropriate triage and treatment. Following the assessment, the therapist must make sure that there is socialization or education of the patient to the treatment model. The ideas of what therapy involves, the goals and plans of the therapy, and the importance of therapeutic collaboration must be stressed. The initial therapeutic focus may be on relieving the presenting symptoms, that is, anxiety or depression. In helping the patient to deal with their anxiety or depression, the therapist can teach the patient the basic cognitive therapy skills that are going to be necessary in working with the more difficult personality disorder. If the therapist can help the patient become less depressed or less anxious the patient may accept that this therapy may have some value after all, and it may be worthwhile continuing to work in therapy.

This book clearly articulates the distinction between the character and temperament dimensions of personality disorders. It then provides a variety of specific, clinically potent interventions for both sets of dimensions. Sperry emphasizes the affective, behavioral, and cognitive temperament "styles" each of us develop. In some cases, the Axis II disorder has been functional in life. Witness the style of the hard-driving executive who was up at 5:00 each morning and worked until 7:00 in the evening (behavioral style). Having worked so hard to be successful, financially secure, and a good provider for his family, he is at a loss to explain his difficulty at retirement. He feels himself to be a failure, on the basis of his lack of productivity (cognitive style). The same schema that drove him to be successful now drive him to depression and despair (affective style).

As another example, a 66-year-old man, diagnosed as both obsessive-compulsive and avoidant (behavioral style), stated, "The best time in my life was when I was in the army. I didn't have to worry about what to wear, what to do, where to go, or what to eat (cognitive style). I was really happy then (affective style)." We know that individuals with dependent personalities are sometimes ideal for service in the military, government bureaucracies, or large corporations because they are compliant with orders and procedures and follow orders well. However, when these styles stop working the individual experiences the depression and anxiety that may prompt their referral for therapy.

Given the difficulties inherent in working with the personality disorders, these patients can profit from therapy. What is essential is that the therapist have a firm theoretical orientation, a reasonable conceptual framework for understanding the individual, and a broad spectrum of cognitive, affective, and behavioral interventions at their disposal. Much of the difficulty has revolved around the lack of a well-defined and articulated approach for treating the individual with a personality disorders. Dr. Sperry has synthesized his broad theoretical base, experience, sensitivity, and a sharp clinical acumen that offers a truly integrative approach to treating individuals with personality disorder. Examining six of the DSM-IV personality disorders, he takes the reader through his clinical thinking in terms of diagnosis, conceptualization, and treatment. Of especial value is the "bridging" nature of this volume. It incorporates psychodynamic, systemic, biological, and cognitive-behavioral formulations. It unashamedly discusses transference and countertransference along with the directive interventions that have demonstrated efficacy and come from the cognitive-behavioral work. Similarly, Sperry discusses the use and value of medication and psychotherapy as cooperative treatments with a goal of treating the patient from a biopsychosocial perspective (rather than as competitive and divisive and treating the patient as a combination of separate and discrete systems).

The real value of this book will be most evident with the more difficult to treat personality-disordered individuals. Sperry provides not only a clinically useful road map of the various phases of the treatment process (engagement, pattern analysis, pattern change, and pattern maintenance), but also an unmatched compilation of treatment resources—individual, group, family, medication, skill training, and combined treatment—all between two covers! This is about as user friendly as a book can be.

Experienced clinicians will appreciate and resonate with the author's general and specific treatment guidelines. For instance, Sperry advocates the use of specific behavioral interventions—sometimes in conjunction with medication—to reasonably modulate a patient's uncontrollable affects (temperament dimension) before attempting to interpret or cognitively restructure (character dimension).

In many ways, this is a comprehensive treatment manual for the treatment of the patient with a personality disorder. It is an approach to the treatment of the personality disorders that is not only based on a sound theoretical framework, but also deftly guides the clinician safely around a variety of potential therapeutic land mines in the treatment process. And it offers the kind of therapeutic strategies that can maximize treatment outcomes. This exciting new book may just set the standard for other treatment texts!

Arthur Freeman, Ed.D.
Co-author, *Cognitive Therapy of the Personality Disorders*

PREFACE

There is a paradigm shift occurring in the treatment of personality disorders. This shift is evidenced in the spate of articles, workshops, courses, and books promoting methods of treating personality disorders with results that were unimaginable even 5 years ago. It is evidenced in the way the personality disorders are being conceptualized today. Whereas the Greeks conceptualized personality in terms of temperament, that is, the four humors, and Freud conceptualized personality in terms of character, today there is increasing research data and clinical experience suggesting that personality and personality disorders are better conceptualized in both temperament *and* character terms.

Yet, this shift is dramatically evidenced by the degree of sophistication in planning and implementing treatment strategies. Consider the following clinical examples.

Two patients present for psychiatric treatment at the same time. Both were attractive single females in their late twenties, both were college graduates, both had similar presenting complaints, and both had the same diagnosis: borderline personality disorder. Beyond these commonalities, they were actually quite different. Most notable was the fact that treatment interventions that were appropriate and effective with one were inappropriate and ineffective with the other.

Keri A. was brought to the emergency room by her boyfriend with agitation, dysphoria, and a laceration to her left wrist. Apparently, her boyfriend was late in returning from an out-of-town business trip and Keri, thinking he was never going to show up for the candlelight dinner she had prepared for him, became increasingly agitated believing he was out with another woman, and slashed her left wrist. He arrived at her apartment 20 minutes later and immediately transported her to the nearest hospital emergency room. This was only the second time in her life that this 28-year-old woman had acted out impulsively. Three years ago she had also lacerated her wrist in similar circumstances with a previous boyfriend. She reported a stable work history for the past 6 years following college graduation. Recently, she was promoted to district manager. Keri described having four relatively close friends, including her roommate, whom she had known since her college days. She apparently relates well with her coworkers, including her male boss. Although she maintains regular contact with her family, she admits that her relationship with her mother is sometimes strained. Her Global Assessment Functioning (GAF) Scale score on admission was 40, with the highest level in the past year estimated at 71. In the emergency room, she received a sedative and had her wrist sutured. After denying suicidal ideation and accepting a referral for outpatient psychiatric treatment, she was discharged and left with her boyfriend. She began weekly treatment sessions later that week. It was her first adult experience with individual therapy, having talked to a counselor in high school a few times after breaking up with a boyfriend. She responded well to a dynamic-oriented therapy, which involved the therapeutic confrontation method described by Masterson (Masterson & Klein, 1989). Treatment was terminated in 42 sessions, spaced over a period of 18 months. Following treatment, she married her boyfriend. In a letter received 2 years later, Keri indicated she and her husband had recently given birth to their first child and that things were going quite well for her.

Cindy J. also presented in the emergency room with wrist lacerations. She had been brought in by an ambulance called by her landlady. Apparently, after having her social security disability check stolen from her mail box and being "dumped"—her words—by her off-again, on-again boyfriend, she proceeded to get drunk and slash both her wrists. In the emergency room, she was so angry and combative that she had to be restrained while her wrists were being sutured. Medical records showed she had a long history of episodes of psychiatric treatment with three psychiatrists and two social workers, including various medication trials and three prior suicide attempts (two involving overdosing on prescribed antidepressants). Compliance with those appointments during those episodes of care as well as compliance with prescribed medications was poor. She noted that following graduation from college—after 7 years of trying various majors—she worked at several jobs. In most of the positions she held, she was underemployed, particularly in the past 3 years. She had started receiving social security disability some 18 months before her latest suicide attempt. She indicated that she had never really gotten along with her family, except for her father. Although she felt quite close to him as a child, he became increasingly emotionally distant from her during her adolescence and continuing to the present. She reported having no real friends, and, except for a small dog, feels rejected by everybody. In the emergency room, her GAF Scale score was estimated to be 28, with her highest level in the previous year at 42. Because she verbalized continued suicidal ideation, she was hospitalized for 3 days and then transitioned into a partial hospitalization program for 6 months, and then subsequently into an outpatient aftercare program where she remains some 3 years later. Because she had failed to respond to individual weekly therapy sessions in the past, she was referred to a partial hospital program with a focused treatment program for severe personality disordered patients. The program consisted of occupational therapy and pre-employment training, medication groups, symptom management groups, social skill training groups, in addition to weekly individual therapy sessions. After 6 months in the program, Cindy's GAF was 56. After 18 months, she was working steadily at a part-time job and continuing in a twice-weekly social skills training and biweekly medication group. Her GAF was then estimated at 68 when she "graduated" to monthly individual sessions consisting of supportive therapy and medication monitor. She began working full-time as a department manager for a large retail store and has continued in that capacity for the past 11 months without any further hospitalizations or suicide gestures.

Besides some obvious similarities of demographics and diagnosis, the psychiatric histories and treatment responses of both of these women are considerably different. Perhaps the most obvious differences were in level of symptomatic distress and level of functioning that reflected the extent of temperament dysregulation and adequacy of coping skills for each woman. Figure P.1 illustrates the extent of temperament dysregulation for three style dimensions: affective style, behavior and relational style, and cognitive style. Clearly, there is significantly more dysregulation or over modulation of the three styles for Cindy than for Keri.

Each responded to very different treatment strategies. Cindy would not and probably could not have responded—at least initially—to the treatment accorded Keri. Nor would it have been appropriate to offer Keri the treatment accorded to Cindy. Of necessity, much of the course of treatment for Cindy emphasized re-modulation of affective, behavioral/relational, and cognitive styles, whereas there was little such emphasis in Keri's treatment. In both instances the treatment strategies used were individualized and tailored to the unique needs and circumstances of each patient.

In other words, these cases illustrate that two similar individuals with the same Axis II diagnosis can and do have different treatment courses and differential responses to treatment interventions. These cases reflect the new way in which a growing number of psychiatric and behavioral health researchers and clinicians are conceptualizing and treating personality disorders today. As a result, there is increasing hope that many, if not most, personality disordered individuals can be effectively treated and managed with focused treatment strategies and interventions. There is also some speculation that "cure" may some day be an expected treatment outcome.

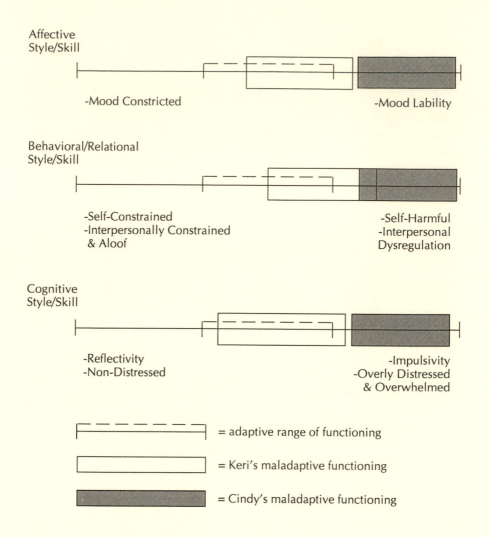

FIGURE P.1.   Style/skill dimensions of borderline personality disorder.

Whereas it was once assumed that treatment even of milder personality disorders required years of intensive psychotherapy, published case reports and even prospective studies are indicating that shorter term treatment can be effective with even severe disorders, such as borderline personality. Yet, it was less than 5 years ago that most clinicians ascribed to the belief that most borderline personality-disordered individuals were untreatable and even unmanageable.

This book is about this paradigm shift and how clinicians can increase their effectiveness and efficacy in working with personality disordered individuals by adopting a focused treatment strategy and tailoring interventions to patient need and severity of the disorder. A basic premise underlying the treatment process and the various intervention strategies proposed in this book is that effective treatment is tailored treatment that is focused on both the temperament and character dimensions of personality and the degree of severity of the disorder. Furthermore, effective treatment often requires the use of treatment modalities above and beyond individual psychotherapy.

This book describes the increasing applicability and effectiveness of a variety of cognitive and behavioral intervention strategies and tactics with personality disordered individuals. The convergence of these two developments seems incredibly serendipitous. Potent cognitive therapy intervention strategies have been quite effective in modifying characterological or schema dimension in personality disordered individuals. Similarly, equally potent behavior therapy intervention strategies have been found to be singularly effective in modifying the temperament or style dimension that accounts for much of the acting out and treatment "resistance" noted in personality disordered individuals.

It highlights both these cognitive and behavioral interventions; it catalogues the maladaptive schemas commonly observed in specific personality disorders; and it describes 15 common structured treatment interventions. Along with these cognitive-behavioral strategies, the book also describes combined use of other strategies such as medication, group, marital and family, and integrative methods. Extended case studies illustrate the use of these various intervention strategies.

This book is divided into two parts. Part I introduces the reader to the paradigm shift that is occurring in psychiatry and behavioral health today, with regard to the treatment of the personality disorders. The three chapters in Part I provide the reader with an understanding and appreciation of both the character and temperament dimensions that are manifest in personality disordered individuals.

Part II describes an integrative and practical approach to the treatment of six personality disorders that are commonly seen in clinical practice. A growing number of clinicians and researchers are of the opinion that *six DSM-IV personality disorders—the avoidant, borderline, dependent, histrionic, narcissistic, and obsessive-compulsive—are considered reasonably "treatable."* Reasonable treatability means that not only can these six disorders be effectively managed in outpatient settings, but in some instances might even be cured (Stone, 1993). The four remaining DSM-IV disorders (schizoid, schizotypal, paranoid, and antisocial personality disorders) are not considered as treatable and are less commonly seen in outpatient settings.

Accordingly, they are not included in this manual. In other words, the most common personality disorders seen in an outpatient setting are also the ones that are most treatable, and these six disorders are detailed in Part II.

The six chapters in Part II provide an easy-to-follow "map" of the treatment process and its various phases: engagement, pattern analysis, pattern change, and termination and pattern maintenance, which includes follow-up and relapse prevention. Although this book emphasizes the usefulness and effectiveness of cognitive-behavioral interventions in the context of individual treatment, various other modalities and intervention strategies are also described. These include medication, group therapy and other group interventions, family interventions, and couples therapy. Case material illustrates the process of treatment for each of these six disorders.

The book is intended as a "hands-on" manual for practicing clinicians as well as clinicians-in-training. It offers clinicians a hopeful perspective on the treatability of these disorders and highly effective treatment protocols for achieving positive treatment outcomes. I trust it will make a difference in the lives of those who are afflicted with these disorders.

AN OVERVIEW

Part I contains three chapters that lay the foundation for use of treatment strategies for specific personality disorders described in Part II.

Chapter 1, "Cognitive-Behavioral Strategies for Effective Treatment of the Personality Disorders: Basic Considerations," describes the paradigm shift that is occurring in the conceptualization, assessment, and treatment of personality disorders today. The implications of this paradigm shift for effective treatment of personality disorder are then articulated in terms of basic premises of clinical intervention and the treatment process itself.

Chapter 2, "Character and Schema Change," describes the character dimension of personality and its evolution and transformation into "schema" language. Schema is discussed with regard to the cognitive-behavioral and psychodynamic traditions, and several schemas commonly noted among personality disordered individuals are described. These schemas will be referred to repeatedly throughout Chapters 4–9.

Chapter 3, "Temperament and Style Change," describes the temperament dimension in personality and its revival in the formulation and treatment of personality disorders. Several specific treatment interventions targeted to modifying temperament or style are described. It seems that clinicians who attempt to provide effective treatment to patients with severe personality disorders must have sufficient capability to use these or similar interventions. Because many of these interventions are not commonly used by clinicians, each is described in some detail—along with a key reference for further study—in Chapter 3. These interventions will be referred to repeatedly throughout Chapters 4–9.

CHAPTER

1

Cognitive-Behavioral Strategies for Effective Treatment of the Personality Disorders: Basic Considerations

Whether or not clinicians are comfortable ascribing paradigm shift language to clinical practice, there is no denying that major changes in the treatment of the personality disorders have and are occurring. These changes involve not only radically different treatment methods, but also rather different theories, conceptualizations, criteria, and assessment methods. Not surprisingly, theoretical speculation about the personality disorders has greatly increased. However, what is surprising is the growing number of theories on personality disorders that are research-based (Clarkin & Lenzenweger, 1996). Language regarding the personality disorders has also dramatically changed.

Before 1980, personality disorders were typically conceptualized in "character language," such as the oral character or obsessive character. Although there was a biological tradition in the study of personality that emphasized temperament, the psychological tradition that emphasized character was in vogue for most of the 20th century. Descriptions of personality disorde-s in DSM-I and DSM-II reflected this emphasis on character and psychodynamics. Within the psychoanalytic community, character reflected specific defense mechanisms. Accordingly, the defense of isolation of affect, intellectualization, and rationalization were common in the obsessive character.

☐ Changes in the Conceptualizations of Personality Disorders

Currently, personality disorders are being conceptualized in a broader perspective that includes both character and temperament. Neurobiological and biosocial formulations of personality disorder have attracted considerable attention and have generated a considerable amount of research. Millon (1996) and Cloninger (1993) hypothesized that temperament and neurotransmitters greatly influence personality development and functioning. Like many others, both Stone (1993), a psychoanalyst, and Cloninger, a neurobiological psychiatrist, described personality as the confluence of both character and temperament.

Character refers to the learned, psychosocial influences on personality. Character forms largely because of the socialization process, particularly regarding cooperativeness, and the mirroring process that promotes the development of self-concept and a sense of purpose in life (i.e., self-transcendence and self-responsibility). Another way of specifying the characterological component of personality is with the term *schema*. Whether in the psychoanalytic tradition (Horowitz, 1988; Slap & Slap-Shelton, 1991) or the cognitive therapy tradition (Beck, 1964; Young, 1990) schema refers to the basic beliefs individuals use to organize their view of self, the world, and the future. Whereas the centrality of schema has historically been more central to the cognitive tradition and the cognitive-behavioral tradition than to the psychoanalytic tradition, this apparently is changing (Stein & Young, 1992). Schema and schema change and modification strategies are central to this book.

Temperament refers to the innate, genetic, and constitutional influences on personality. Whereas character and schema reflect the psychological dimension of personality, temperament (or style, as it is used synonymously in this book) reflects the biological dimension of personality. Cloninger et al. (1993) contended that temperament has four biological dimensions (novelty-seeking, harm-avoidance, reward-dependence, and persistence), whereas character has three quantifiable dimensions (self-directedness or self-responsibility, cooperativeness, and self-transcendence). Other researchers would describe impulsivity and aggressivity as additional dimensions of temperament (Costello, 1996).

Temperament and character can be assessed by interviews and self-report instruments. The relevance of distinguishing character and temperament for treatment planning is significant. Whereas insight-oriented psychotherapy might be focused on the character dimensions, psychotherapy will have little or no impact on temperament dimensions. For example, in the case of Cindy where dysregulation of temperament was significant (i.e., her impulsivity, harm avoidance, and aggressivity), neither medications nor individual psychotherapy were sufficient to effect change. However, the addition of focused skill training and the structured milieu of the partial hospitalization program were necessary to sufficiently regulate or modulate her effects and behaviors so that she could then profit from individual and group therapy directed at the character dimensions. On the other hand, Keri's temperament was sufficiently modulated such that psychotherapy could be the principal treatment directed primarily at the character issues.

☐ Changes in the Criteria for Personality Disorders

In the past, criteria for the personality disorders were somewhat primitive. DSM-I categorized the personality disorder into five headings: personality pattern disturbance, personality trait disturbance, sociopathic personality disturbance, special symptom reactions, and transient situational personality disorders. DSM-II, which appeared in 1968, eliminated the subheading and streamlined the number of personality disorders; however, the descriptions were not based on clinical trials. Although brief descriptions of each disorder were given, diagnostic criteria were not provided. Furthermore, there was no clear distinction made between symptom disorders (Axis I) and personality disorders (Axis II). This lack of specificity also reinforced some mistaken notions about personality disorders. A notable example is obsessive-compulsive disorder and obsessive-compulsive personality disorder. Prior to DSM-III, no distinction was made between these disorders, whereas today there is general consensus that these disorders have relatively little overlap (Jenike, 1991). This belief about the inherent similarity of these disorders may be attributable to Freud's formulation of the case of the Rat Man in which both obsessive-compulsive disorder and obsessive-compulsive personality disorder happened to be comorbid conditions. The implication was that both are essentially the same, and so treatment should be the same for both disorders. Jenike noted that the concurrence of obsessive-compulsive disorder in patients with obsessive-compulsive personality disorder is small, probably less than 15–18%.

The criteria for DSM-IV have been considerably refined over those for DSM-III. Although these criteria are useful in ruling in or ruling out a personality disorder, they are not particularly useful in planning treatment (Stone, 1993). For one thing, there is no weight given to specific criteria. For another, some criteria seem to reflect character features of the disorder whereas other criteria reflect temperament features, but because they are not so identified or weighted they have little value in formulating treatment. For instance, the nine criteria for borderline personality disorder seem to reflect four temperament features—#4 and #5 involving dysregulated cognitive style (impulsivity), #6 and #8 involving dysregulated affective style—whereas the others reflect character features. DSM-IV requires that *any* five or more criteria are needed to rule in the diagnosis of borderline personality disorder, irrespective of whether they reflect character or temperament features. This lack of specificity is unfortunate.

Reviewing the cases of Keri and Cindy presented in the Introduction, Keri would be found to meet four character criteria and possibly only one temperament criteria (#5), although her wrist-cutting could hardly be considered recurrent suicidal behavior. On the other hand, Cindy met all four of the temperament criteria and three of the character criteria. Parenthetically, few would disagree that Cindy's treatment will be much more complex and challenging than Keri's, largely because of the difficultly modulating impulsivity, mood lability, and angry outbursts that reflect temperament. In short, it would be clinically useful for future editions of the DSM to weight and specify criteria.

☐ Changes in the Assessment of Personality Disorders

In the past, assessment of personality disorder was by clinical interview and inferred from standardized personality inventories like the MMPI (Millon, 1996). Today, there are a number of formal measures of personality disorders. Some are theory- and research-based such as Cloninger's (1993) Temperament Character Inventory (TCI). There are a number of semistructured schedules available such as the Structured Clinical Interview for DSM-III-R Personality Disorders (SCID-II).

In large part, these assessment measures reflect the increasingly differentiated criteria of DSM-III, DSM-III-R, and DSM-IV. DSM-III subdivided 11 personality disorders—antisocial, avoidant, borderline, compulsive, dependent, histrionic, narcissistic, paranoid, passive-aggressive, schizoid, and schizotypal—into three clusters: odd, dramatic, and anxious. DSM-III-R maintained the essential features of DSM-III but added the sadistic and self-defeating personality disorders to the appendix. DSM-IV further differentiated criteria and dropped the self-defeating and sadistic personality disorders. It relegated passive-aggressive personality disorder to the personality disorder category not otherwise specified (NOS), as well as depressive personality disorder, which joined passive-aggressive personality disorder in Appendix B of DSM-IV.

☐ Changes in the Treatment of Personality Disorders

In the past, the treatment of personality disorders was largely the domain of psychodynamic approaches. Psychoanalysis and long-term psychoanalytically oriented psychotherapy were considered the treatment of choice (Stone, 1993). The goal of treatment was to change character structure. Unfortunately, outcomes were mixed even among patients judged amenable to treatment. For the most part, clinicians using a traditional exploratory approach adopted a neutral and passive stance and primarily used clarification and interpretation strategies.

Treatment methods today are considerably different in that treatment tends to be more focused and structured, with the clinician taking a more active role (Beitman, 1991; Millon, 1996; Stone, 1993; Sperry, 1995a). Many of these treatment approaches and intervention strategies are theory-based and have been researched in clinical trials in comparison with other treatment approaches or other modalities such as medication, group therapy, or family therapy. The cognitive therapy approach (Beck, Freeman, & Associates, 1990), the interpersonal psychotherapy approach (Benjamin, 1993), and some psychodynamic approaches (Stone, 1996) have been specifically modified for the treatment of personality disordered individuals.

Psychopharmacological research on treatment of selected personality disorders has grown rapidly in the past few years (Silk, 1996; Sperry, 1995b). Until very recently, the consensus among clinicians was that medication didn't and couldn't treat personality disorders, per se, but rather concurrent Axis I conditions or target symptoms like insomnia. This view is rapidly changing. Essentially, a growing number of psychopharmacologists believe that psychopharmacological treatment can and should be directed to basic dimensions that underlie the personality (Siever & Davis, 1991; Silk, 1996; Sperry, 1995b). Specifically, a psychobiological treatment model, based on the biological correlates of personality disorders, proposed by Siever and Davis has considerable clinical and research promise. The model consists of four dimensions: (a) cognitive/perceptual organizations, especially for the schizotypal and passive disorders for which low dose neuroleptics might be useful; (b) impulsivity and aggression, in the borderline and antisocial for which serotonin blockers can be useful; (c) affective instability, for borderline and histrionic personalities for which cyclic antidepressants or serotonin blockers may be useful; and (d) anxiety/inhibition, particularly in the avoidant personalty disorder for which serotonin blockers and MAOI agents may be useful (Siever & Davis, 1991).

There is growing consensus, among all segments of the psychiatric community, that effective treatment of the personality disorders involves combining treatment modalities and integrating treatment approaches (Sperry, 1995a). This includes psychoanalytically oriented psychiatrists who advocate combined treatment, particularly for severe personality disorders (Gabbard, 1994; Stone, 1993; Winer & Pollock, 1989). Stone suggested combining three approaches: supportive interventions, which are particularly useful in fostering a therapeutic alliance and should be augmented by psychoanalytic interventions, which are useful in resolving negative transferences at the outset of treatment, and cognitive-behavioral interventions, which are useful in the development of new attitudes and habits. Combining medication with individual and group modalities can also increase effectiveness. Such efforts to integrate various approaches, as well as to combine treatment modalities, would have been considered heretical just a few years ago. Now, integrating and combining treatments is an emerging consensus that reflects the immensity of the "paradigm shift" that is occurring (Beitman, 1991; Sperry, 1995a).

☐ Basic Premises About Effective Treatment of Personality Disorders

The paradigm shift in clinicians' attitudes and practice styles regarding personality disorders was discussed in terms of conceptualizations, assessment, and treatment. Consistent with this paradigm shift, this book provides a number of specific effective intervention strategies based on the following premises.

Premise #1: Maximizing Readiness for Change Is Essential in the Effective Treatment of Personality Disorders

A patient's readiness for treatment and level of functioning reflects their treatability and prognosis (Sperry, 1995a). As will be described in more detail later in this chapter, *patient readiness* refers to the individual patient's motivation for and expectations for treatment outcomes—which can be assessed in terms of four levels—as well as past history of treatment compliance and success at efforts to change habits and behavior patterns. Level of functioning can be operationalized in terms of Global Assessment of Functioning (GAF) Scale of Axis IV. High functioning refers to a score of about 65. Moderate functioning refers to scores of 45–65. Low functioning refers to scores below 45.

Personality disorders can be classified in terms of *treatability*: (a) *high amenability* includes the dependent, histrionic, obsessive-compulsive, avoidant, and depressive personality disorders; (b) *intermediate amenability* includes narcissistic, borderline, and schizotypal personality disorders; and (c) *low-amenability* includes paranoid, passive aggressive, schizoid, and antisocial personality disorders (Stone, 1993). Stone added that because patients show mixtures of various personality features or disorders, prognosis is largely dependent on the degree to which features of the disorders in the third category are present. Prognosis will also depend in part on the prominence of the psychobiological dimensions described by Siever and Davis (1991): cognitive/perceptual disorganization; impulsivity/aggression, and affective instability or anxiety/inhibition. To the extent that dimensions like impulsivity or anxiety respond to medication, concurrent psychosocial intervention efforts should be facilitated.

Premise #2: Combined, Tailored, and Integrative Treatment Modalities Become Increasingly Necessary the Lower the Level of Treatability

Combined treatment refers to adding modalities, such as individual, group, couple, or family, either concurrently or sequentially, whereas *integrative treatment* refers to the blending of different treatment approaches or orientation, such as psychodynamic, cognitive, behavioral, interpersonal, and the like. *Tailored treatment* refers to specific ways of customizing treatment modalities and/or therapeutic approaches to "fit" the unique needs, cognitive and emotional styles, and treatment expectations of the patient. Treatments delivered in combination can have an additive, and sometimes synergistic, effect.

The higher the patient's treatability, the less need or immediacy there may be for combining and blending most of the modalities and approaches. On the other hand, the lower the level of treatability, the more that modalities and approaches will need to be combined and blended.

Premise #3: Effective Treatment of the Personality Disorders Is Guided by General and Specific Treatment Goals

General treatment goals involving the personality disorders can be specified in four levels. First-level goals involve reducing symptoms. Second-level goals involve modulating the temperament dimension of personality. Third-level goals involve reducing impaired social, occupational, and relational functioning. Finally, fourth-level goals involve modifying the character or schema dimension of personality. It should be noted that Level 2 and 4 goals involve modification rather than radical restructuring. Stone (1993) used the analogy of the cabinet maker and carpenter to illustrate treatment goals regarding character and temperament. He likened the clinician working with personality disordered individuals to a cabinet maker who sands down the rough edges of a structure rather than a carpenter who rebuilds the structure. The patient's character and temperament remain, but treatment renders the individual somewhat easier with which to work or live.

Achieving Level 1 and 3 goals are easier than Level 2 and 4 goals. Medication and/or behavioral treatments like exposure or thought stopping may quickly remit symptoms. Advice, limit setting, encouragement, and environmental restructuring are often useful in achieving higher levels of life functioning. Perhaps the most challenging and time-intensive aspect of treatment of personality disorders involves modifying character and modulating temperament. Psychotherapeutic interventions are principally used for modifying character, whereas medication and skill training have been more effective in modulating temperament.

Both clinical experience (Freeman & Davison, 1997; Sperry, 1995a) and research (Linehan, Heard, & Armstrong, 1993) suggest that modulation of temperament or styles must come before modification of character structure or schemas. *Modulation* refers to normalizing affective, behavioral, and/or cognitive style or responsivity that is either excessive or insufficient. Usually, this strategy is required with lower functioning personality disordered individuals because their under- or overmodulated temperament and acting out style renders them unready and unprepared for therapies oriented to character modification. It is only when their temperament is adequately modulated that they will have sufficient self-restraint and resources to profit from standard psychotherapies. Attempting to modify character before modulating temperament can result in negative therapeutic reactions. The patient will either act out or regress, often leading to rehospitalization. The prototypical example is the articulate but lower-to-moderate functioning borderline patient who insists on or goes along with the clinician's desire to process early abuse issues. Soon there-after, the clinician is surprised when the patient becomes preoccupied with suicidal thoughts or has significantly regressed so that hospitalization is needed (Linehan, 1993). The initial goal of Linehan's dialectical behavior therapy with borderline patients is to achieve an adequate degree of modulation such that the patients are more disposed to ongoing treatment. Linehan utilized various interventions to modulate patients' affective lability, impulsiveness, and parasuicidal and other acting-out behaviors before shifting the focus to more characterological issues. Her research—a prospective study—indicates that this treatment strategy was significantly better in reducing rehospitalization and parasuicidality and treatment drop-out than traditional treatment (Linehan, Heard, & Armstrong, 1993).

Effective treatment of the personality disorders is guided not only by general treatment goals but also by specific treatment goals, which will be elaborated on in Chapters 4–9. These specific goals address specific treatment targets. For example, take schema change. In cognitive therapy, specific treatment goals can be stated in terms of the level of schema change possible or desirable. There are four levels of schema change. Schema change can range from the maximal level of change, which is called "schema reconstruction," to "schema camouflage," which is the minimal level of change (Beck, Freeman, & Associates, 1990). These four levels and their treatment indications and implications are detailed in Chapter 2.

Premise #4: When a Patient Presents with More Than One Personality Disorder, Each Disorder Is Initially Treated Separately

It is not unusual for patients to present with two or more personality disorders (Millon, 1996). In such instances, the manifestations of each disorder usually do not occur simultaneously nor are the features of the disorders blended. In other words, the characterological and temperament or style manifestations of two personality disorders are more like a chocolate-vanilla swirled cone than a mixture of the colors red and yellow that yield the color orange. In other words, both disorders are relatively discrete and intact at any one time.

For example, in the early phases of treatment the clinician who is working with an individual who meets criteria for both obsessive-compulsive personality disorder and narcissistic personality disorder will observe the characteristic drivenness and ambivalence of the obsessive-compulsive personality at some points in the session, and minutes later the entitlement and grandiosity of the narcissistic personality may be evidenced.

A suggested overall treatment strategy in working with patients with more than one personality disorder is to focus principally on the character and temperament/style features of the more distressing or troubling disorder. As manifestations of the other disorder(s) are operative, deal with them and then return to the principal focus. A marker of real change in treatment is that the separate manifestations of the different disorders become less pronounced to the point where the now-muted features of those disorders appear to blend.

For didactic purposes, it has been necessary to focus the chapters of this book—and the case examples cited—on single disorders. Because it is common for individuals to present with more than one personality disorder, it does not mean that effective treatment is not achievable or requires considerably more time or expertise. Rather, the clinician need only attend to this premise and focus treatment on the predominant disorder recognizing that when manifestations of the other disorder(s) arise they are recognized and dealt with accordingly.

☐ An Effective Treatment Strategy for Personality Disorders

The treatment strategy proposed in this book is rather straightforward. Treatment must be specifically planned with regard to the four stages of the treatment process, and it must be specifically tailored on the basis of the patient's needs, style, level of readiness, and expectations of treatment. This section describes the stages of the treatment process and tailoring treatment.

Stages of the Treatment Process

The process of change and the types of interventions required for the effective treatment of the personality disorders is similar to the general therapeutic processes and interventions used with symptom disorders, but it differs in focus and emphasis. Beitman (1991) has articulated the general change processes and compatible interventions in both psychotherapy and psychopharmacotherapy. The Beitman model articulates four developmental stages of the treatment process: engagement, pattern search, change, and termination. As applied to the treatment of personality disorders, these stages need to be somewhat modified. The stages of engagement, pattern identification, pattern change, and pattern maintenance are described below and will be illustrated in subsequent chapters with regard to specific personality disorders.

Engagement.   Engagement is the principal therapeutic process in the early phase of treatment. Engagement requires the patient to trust, respect, and accept the influence of the provider. The building of trust and respect results in psychological connection and commitment. The provider's empathic stance toward the patient is essential in establishing a working therapeutic relationship or therapeutic bond. Engagement is a prelude to psychotherapy and psychopharmacotherapy, and until it is achieved little if any change is possible. This is not to say that unengaged patients will not attend sessions—they might—but there is little likelihood that any positive movement will occur. One early indication that engagement has been achieved is the patient's willingness to collaborate and take increasing responsibility for making necessary changes in their lives.

By definition, collaboration means that both parties, not just one, take responsibility. It is for this reason that, from the very outset, the clinician must ensure that the first task of treatment is to develop a collaborative working relationship. In such a relationship, both clinician and patient agree to focus their energies on the same treatment goals and objectives. It is the patient's responsibility to pursue the mutually agreed on goals and objectives. And, when patients sidestep or move away from an agreed upon goal, it is the clinician's responsibility to confront the diversion. Therapeutic confrontation is used to return to the treatment goal and refocus the patient on the here and now of the therapeutic transaction. The clinician might say: "Wait a minute! What's going on between us that *we* ended up here? *We* agreed to work on _____. What happened?" Emphasizing "we" is crucial in a collaborative effort because both need to accept responsibility. Typically, the manner in which the borderline patient deviates and moves away from the agreed on treatment goal or objective then becomes the focus itself. Thoughts or discussion about a troubling relationship or a failure to achieve personal goals will result in a move away from goal to the extent they feel threatened. The clinician processes the focus sufficiently until goals are sufficiently realigned. By definition, personality disordered individuals find it difficult to cooperate and collaborate much less take responsibility for their own behavior.

Engagement involves a socialization process that culminates in a formal or informal treatment contract and includes elements such as fee, length of sessions, and duration of treatment, and education about the treatment process. Even more important is clarification and negotiation of expectations, goals, and role behaviors and responsibilities for both patient and clinician for the treatment process.

A critical task of the engagement stage is to assess the patient's readiness and motivation for treatment and, if necessary, increase it. Four levels of readiness for change can be noted (Prochaska & DiClementi, 1982). They are *precontemplation*, which means the patient denies illness or any need for treatment; *contemplation*, which means that though the patient accepts that they have an illness and may need treatment for it, they have not decided to make changes; *action*, which means the individual has decided to and has begun making changes; and *maintenance*, which means sustaining the change and preventing relapse. Low readiness for treatment is noted in precontemplation and contemplation. It will be reflected in treatment resistance and noncompliance in various ways: missing or coming late for appointments, failure to take medication or complete intersession assignment, or minimal or no progress in treatment. If the patient does not possess sufficient treatment readiness, the provider's task is to focus on the readiness issue before proceeding with formal psychotherapy or psychopharmacotherapy. Motivational counseling is a potent strategy for increasing readiness for change (Miller & Rollnick, 1991).

Predictably, transference and countertransference issues emerge in the engagement stage in subtle and not-so-subtle ways. This is particularly true in the treatment of personality disordered individuals. In the following chapter, transference and countertransference issues for specific personality disorders are noted along with suggested intervention strategies.

Pattern Analysis.   Pattern identification involves the elucidation of the patient's maladaptive pattern that reflects their manner of thinking, acting, feeling, coping, and defending self. In the context of this book, *pattern analysis* refers to the patient's specific schemas or characterological features, styles or temperament features, pattern triggers, and levels of functioning and readiness for change. Various assessment strategies can be used to specify the pattern. These include a functional evaluation interview, personality testing and the elicitation of early recollection or core schemas. To the extent that the clinician understands and appreciates this formulation—particularly the predisposing factors and perpetuating factors unique to the patient—confrontation tactics, interpretations, cognitive restructuring, and behavioral interventions will tend to be more focused and efficacious.

Pattern Change.   The purpose of defining underlying maladaptive patterns is to modify or change them. With personality disordered individuals, the therapeutic change focus must, of necessity, include both schemas and styles. The treatment goal and process of therapeutic change involves three tasks: (a) the disordered or maladaptive pattern is relinquished; (b) a more adaptive pattern is adopted; and (c) the new pattern is generalized—

thoughts, feelings, and actions—and maintained. The general treatment strategy is to effect sufficient change or modulation in styles *before* attempting to change or modify schemas. Specific strategies for pattern change target specific disordered styles and schemas.

Disordered or maladaptive schemas are enduring, inflexible, and pervasive core beliefs about self and the world that greatly impact thoughts, beliefs, and behaviors. The goal of treatment is to effect some measure of change in these beliefs such that they are more flexible and functional. Treatment can either restructure, modify, or reinterpret schemas (Layden, Newman, Freeman & Morse, 1993).

Disordered styles are either undermodulated or overmodulated, and the goal of treatment is to achieve some measure of modulation. The styles are unmodulated both because of temperament and failure to learn sufficient self-control. Self-control involves a number of personal and interpersonal skills necessary to function in day-to-day circumstances with some degree of competence. It is necessary to teach the patient the concept of modulation in the context of overmodulation and undermodulation. *Modulation* is the state in which thought precedes action, in which spontaneity is experienced without pretense or exaggeration, and in which coping with problems can lead to effective and responsible behavior.

Needless to say, many personality disordered individuals never adequately learned these skills during their formative years. Thus, it is often necessary to reverse these specific skill deficits in the context of treatment. Either within an individual or group treatment context, these skills are learned and practiced.

Pattern Maintenance.   As the new pattern becomes fixed in the patient's life, the issue of preventing relapse and recurrence needs to be addressed. As formal treatment sessions become less necessary, the issue of termination becomes the therapeutic focus. The elements of the termination process are relatively predictable when contrasted with the wide range of possibilities inherent in the pattern identification and change stages. Patients—and providers—often have difficulty with separation. New symptoms or old ones may appear, prompting requests for additional sessions. Presumably, when difficulty with separation or abandonment is noted in the maladaptive pattern, treatment will have focused on this issue.

Tailoring Treatment

Tailoring treatment involves making treatment selection decisions that provide a reasonably good "fit" between the patient's needs, style, level of readiness and treatment expectations, and available therapeutic resources.

A basic premise of this book is that the lower the patient's level of treatability, the more treatment must be tailored.

According to Frances, Clarkin, and Perry (1984), the process of treatment selection, no matter how divergent in theory or style, involves decision making in five domains. These domains are setting, format, time, approach, and somatic treatment. *Setting* refers to the place in which treatment occurs: inpatient, outpatient clinic or private office, day hospital, or a residential treatment center. *Format* indicates the context of treatment and is a function of who directly participates in the treatment: individual, group, family, couple, medication monitoring or some combination of these modalities such as: individual–medication, individual–group, individual–couple, medication–group, or even individual–couple–medication. *Time* refers to the length and frequency of sessions as well as the duration of treatment. Duration of treatment might be brief or long term, time-limited, open-ended, or discontinuous. Sessions might be scheduled two or more times per week, weekly, biweekly, monthly, bimonthly, or less often. *Approach* refers to the treatment orientation and treatment methods and strategies used by the provider. These range from dynamic to cognitive-behavioral to psychoeducational or supportive. *Somatic* treatments typically refer to psychotropic medications or electroconvulsive therapy but also can include nutritional counseling, or an exercise prescription, or referral for psychosurgery.

The provider also has a metadecision that overrides the consideration of these five components. That is, should any treatment be provided or should "no treatment" be the recommendation of choice? Frances, Clarkin, and Perry (1984) specified the types of patients at risk for negative therapeutic reaction in comparison to those at risk for no response to treatment. They also describe the relative indications for the "no treatment" option. Not surprisingly, they indicate that the "no treatment" option is most often appropriate for severe personality disordered patients, particularly those with a diagnosis of borderline personality disorder.

Tailored treatment often involves combining treatment modalities and approaches. Treatments delivered in combination can have an additive, and sometimes synergistic, effect. It is becoming more evident that different treatment approaches are differentially effective in resolving different types of symptom clusters. For example, in major depression, medication is more effective in remitting vegetative symptoms, whereas psychotherapy is better at improving interpersonal relations and cognitive symptoms.

☐ Summary

This chapter has discussed some of the ferment that is occuring in the treatment of the personality disorders. This discussion has emphasized changes in the conceptualization, assessment, and treatment of Axis II disorders. Conceptualizing and assessing personality disorders in terms of the dual dimensions of character and temperament set the stage for intro-ducing the cognitive-behavioral approach to schema or character change and style or temperament change. The chapter then articulated four basic premises for the effective treatment of personality disorders in an outpa-tient setting. On the basis of these premises, a treatment strategy that de-lineates a four-stage approach—engagement, pattern analysis, pattern change, and pattern maintenance—was described. Finally, a second facet of this treatment strategy, tailoring, was briefly described. Chapters 4–9 illustrate both aspects of this treatment strategy for specific personality disorders.

Character and Schema Change

Character refers to the learned, psychosocial influences on personality. Because character is essentially learned, it follows that it can be changed through such processes as psychotherapy. Largely because of the influence of Freud and his followers, psychotherapy and psychiatric treatment focused almost exclusively on the dimension of character to the point at which personality essentially became synonymous with character. Character forms largely because of the socialization process, particularly regarding cooperativeness, and the mirroring process that promotes the development of self-concept and a sense of purpose in life (i.e., self-transcendence and self-responsibility). Character can be assessed both by structured interview and by self-report inventories. On the Temperament Character Inventory (Cloninger, 1993), character is measured by three character dimensions: cooperativeness, self-directedness—also called self-responsibility—and self-transcendence. Healthy personality reflects plus positive or elevated scores on these three dimensions, whereas personality disorders reflect negative or low scores on them. Furthermore, individuals with low scores on one or more of the character dimensions and increased dysregulation of one or more of the temperament dimensions typically experience either considerable distress or impairment in life functioning or both. For example, the borderline personality disorder would likely rate high in two temperament dimensions but low in character dimensions of self-directedness and cooperation.

☐ Schema

Another way of specifying the characterological component of personality is with term *schema*. Whether in the psychoanalytic tradition (Horowitz, 1988; Slap & Slap-Shelton, 1981) or the cognitive therapy tradition (Beck, 1964; Young, 1994), schema refers to the basic beliefs individuals use to organize their view of self, the world, and the future. Although the centrality of schema has historically been more central to the cognitive tradition and the cognitive-behavioral tradition than to the psychoanalytic tradition, this apparently is changing (Stein & Young, 1992). Schema and schema change and modification strategies are central to this book. The remainder of this chapter reviews some different conceptualizations of schema and then describes several different schemas useful in clinical practice.

Adler first used the term *schema of apperception* in 1929 to refer to the individual's view of self and the world. For Adler, psychopathology reflected the individual's "neurotic schema" (Adler, 1956, p. 333) and these schemas were central to the indiidual's life-style. Recently, the use of the term *schema* and *schema theory* has emerged as central in the various subdisciplines of cognitive science, as well as by various psychotherapy schools' (Stein & Young, 1992) convictions. This section describes the psychodynamic and cognitive-behavioral traditions of schemas.

Psychodynamic Tradition

Whereas classical psychoanalysts focused on libidinal drives, modern analysts have focused instead on relational themes, emphasizing the self, the object, and their interaction, while a number of ego psychology and object relations theorists have emphasized schema theory. Many have contributed to the development of schema theories in the psychoanalytic tradition (Eagle, 1986; Horowitz, 1988; Inderbitzin & James,1994; Slap & Slap-Shelton, 1981; Wachtel, 1982).

A representative example of these theories is the model described by Slap and Slap-Shelton (1991). They described a schema model that contrasts with the structural model devised by Freud and refined by the ego psychologists, and that they contend better fits the clinical data of psychoanalysis than the structural model. Their schema model involves the ego and sequestered schema. The ego consists of many schemas that are loosely linked and integrated with one another and relativity accessible to consciousness. These schemas are based on past experience but are modified by new experience. This process forms the basis of adaptive behavior. Sequestered schemas are organized around traumatic events and situations in childhood that were not mastered or integrated by the immature psyche of the child. These schema remain latent and repressed. To the extent that these sequestered or pathological schemas are active, current relationships may be cognitively processed according to these schemas, rather than treated objectively by the more adaptive schemas of the ego. Essentially, current situations cannot be perceived and processed in accord with the reality of the present event but rather as replications of unmastered childhood conflict.

Treatment consists of helping the patient to describe, clarify, and work through these sequestered, pathological schema. These schemas are exposed to the client's mature, adaptive ego to achieve integration. Patients are helped to recognize how they create and recreate scenarios that reopen their pathologic schemas. The repeated demonstration and working through of the traumatic events that gave rise to the pathological schemas engenders a greater degree of self-observation, understanding, and emotional growth.

Cognitive-Behavioral Tradition

Like the psychodynamic tradition, the cognitive-behavioral tradition is quite heterogeneous. Common to this tradition is the belief that behavior and cognitions influence each other. Approaches within this tradition include stress-inoculation and self-instructional training (Meichenbaum, 1977), rational emotive therapy (Ellis, 1979), and cognitive therapy (Beck, 1976). Because cognitive therapy has taken the lead in articulating schema theory in the cognitive-behavioral tradition, it will be highlighted.

The Basics of Cognitive Therapy.   Cognitive therapy is a relatively recent therapeutic approach developed by a University of Pennsylvania psychiatry professor, Aaron Beck (1976). Although Beck was trained as a psychoanalyst, he was greatly influenced by the work of Adler, Horney, and Rank. Accordingly, there are influences of these cognitively oriented approaches in his system. Beck believes that cognitive processes influence behavior and that overt behavior and emotional expression can be changed by cognitive interventions. Specifically, cognitive therapy aims at altering underlying assumptions that influence a patient's perceptual view, which leads to negative automatic beliefs and dysfunctional cognitions on which behavior is based. In cognitive therapy, the clinician helps the patient to understand and then to modify *automatic thoughts*, *dysfunctional cognitions*, and *core maladaptive schemas*. Examples of automatic thinking are over-

generalization, selective abstraction, minimal evidence, personalization, magnification, and dichotomized or "either-or" thinking, such as "I'll never be good enough" and "People are only nice to you to gain an advantage." Schemas are the silent, core assumptions based on the patient's early experiences that determine the content of cognitions. They form the basis for evaluating, categorizing, and distorting experiences. These thoughts often involve arbitrary conclusions based on what Beck calls automatic thinking.

The treatment process in cognitive therapy is relatively straightforward: The clinician engages the patient as a collaborator in examining her dysfunctional cognitions and how they might be altered. Typically, the patient is asked to keep a daily record of dysfunctional thoughts. The clinician's role is to challenge these dysfunctional cognitions, the automatic thinking they engender, as well as the schemas that underlie them, so that they can be replaced with more functional cognitions. By modeling this process, the clinician teaches the patient to be able to discover and challenge dysfunctional patterns and to develop more adaptive patterns of thinking and behaving. If treatment is successful, the patient is on her way to becoming her own therapist. Essentially, then, the clinician's role is that of a coach or guide, rather than an expert or guru. A variety of cognitive restructuring techniques, as well as role playing, cognitive rehearsal and other cognitive-behavioral interventions are used. Homework or other between-session assignments are commonly prescribed. Medication may be used in combination with individual cognitive therapy sessions. Other modalities such as group, family, or couples interventions might also be integrated or serve as the primary modality.

Cognitive therapy was originally developed for the treatment of major depression. Over time, it has been adapted for the treatment of the anxiety disorders, substance disorders, psychotic disorders, as well as for the personality disorders. Usually, the course of treatment for depression and anxiety disorders would be 12–20 sessions, whereas treatment of personality disorders could take a year or more (Beck & Freeman, 1990).

Schema Theory in Cognitive Therapy.   Beck introduced the schema concept with reference to depression (Beck, 1964) over 30 years ago, when he described the cognitive triad of depression as negative views of the self, the world, and the future. He describes schemas by types: cognitive, affective, motivational, instrumental, or control schemas. Of these, the most clinically useful are the cognitive schemas regarding self-evaluation and world view or evaluation of others. Beck's colleagues have greatly extended schema theory, specifically with regard to personality disorders (Beck, Freeman, & Associates, 1990; Young, 1990). Young articulated the concept of early maladaptive schemas (EMS) and has described several core schemas commonly noted in individuals with personality disorders. Furthermore, he has developed an assessment instrument for eliciting EMS.

☐ Schema Assessment

There are various ways of assessing schemas. Basic to a schema is the individual's self-view and world view. From an Adlerian perspective, schemas are central to an individual's lifestyle (Adler, 1956). Lifestyle, as well as schemas, can be assessed with a semi-structured interview that includes the elicitation of early recollections or early memories. The process begins by asking the patient: "What is your earliest memory?" or "Think back as far as you can and tell me the first thing you remember." An early recollection must be distinguished from a report. An *early recollection* is a single, specific event that is personally remembered by the individual, whereas a *report* can be an event that occurred more than once or for which the patient was told about the event by another, or by seeing it in a photo, home movie, or video. Additional memories from early and middle childhood are then elicited. From these memories the clinician searches for patterns related to the patient's view of self, that is, "I am strong, defective, unloved," and the patient's view of the world: "The world puts too many demands on me, is a scary place, is unfair." These views can be summarized and interpreted to reveal the individual's lifestyle themes or schemas (Eckstein, Baruth, & Mahrer, 1992). The case studies in Chapters 8 and 9 illustrate how early recollections are interpreted as schemas.

In the cognitive therapy tradition, schemas are typically identified or derived from the interview process (Beck, Freeman, & Associates, 1990). Young (1994) briefly described his approach to schema identification: The evaluation interview is critical in identifying schemas. In this interview, the clinician elicits presenting symptoms and problems and attempts to formulate a connection between specific symptoms, emotions, life problems, and maladaptive schemas.

During the course of inquiry about life events and symptoms, the clinician endeavors to develop hypotheses about patterns or themes. Issues of autonomy, connectedness, worthiness, reasonable expectations, and realistic limits are probed to ascertain if any of these present significant problems for the patient. It can be quite useful to inquire about "critical incidents" by asking the patient to describe a situation or incident that they consider indicative of their problem (Freeman, 1992). The clinician listens for specific triggers, patterns indicative of schemas, and specific behavioral, emotional, and cognitive responses. As themes and patterns emerge, the clinician formulates them in schema language, that is, view of self and view of the world and others. Because schemas are predictable and recurring phenomenon they can be "triggered" in the interview through imagery and discussing upsetting events in past or present. This process of triggering confirms the clinician's hypothesis about the presence of a specific schema.

In addition, Jeffrey Young and Gary Brown have developed a 123-item self-report instrument for assessing 15 common maladaptive schemas called the Schema Questionnaire (Young, 1994). This questionaire has been validated on both clinical and nonclinical populations (Schmidt et al., 1995).

☐ Schema Change

From a cognitive therapy perspective, schema change is the domain of what has come to be called *schema-focused cognitive therapy*. This approach involves a collaborative process in which the clinician and patient endeavor to understand and alleviate long-term characterological problems. It uses many of the intervention strategies and tactics of short-term cognitive therapy, but it also incorporates a variety of interpersonal and experiential intervention strategies and tactics that assist patients in reexperiencing and distancing themselves from early childhood traumas and wounds.

Schema change involves three steps: (a) identify maladaptive schemas; (b) establish the goal of treatment, that is, the level of schema change; and (c) develop an intervention strategy to accomplish this goal.

Schemas are identified by taking a patient's detailed history and by the Schema Questionnaire (Young, 1994). The purpose is to ascertain the developmental roots of these maladaptive schemas.

The second step is to establish the goal of treatment in terms of degree or level of schema change. Beck et al. (1990) identified schema change in terms of a continuum or levels of change ranging from maximum schema changes to minimal schema change. Four levels can be described.

The first level is *schema reconstruction*. It involves identifying faulty schemas and replacing them with more functional schemas. An example of successful schema reconstruction would be a paranoid personality disordered individual who was transformed into a more trusting person (Beck et al., 1990). Such total change may not be possible or feasible in that not all dysfunctional schemas can be restructured nor are all patients capable of undergoing such major change. Although many clinicians might look to this level of change as the ideal therapeutic goal, it can seldom be achieved (Freeman & Davison, 1997).

The second level is *schema modification*. It is analogous to rehabilitating a house and involves identifying schemas and modifying rather than replacing them. An example of schematic modification would involve modification of the schema: "I must always have others around if I'm going to survive" to "I must generally have others around for me to survive." Although the schema has not changed completely, the absolutistic nature of it is greatly modified (Freeman & Davison, 1997).

The third level is *reinterpretation*. This involves helping the patient to use an existing schema in a more prosocial way. For example, an excitement-seeking schema would be reframed as potentially adaptive rather than simply maladaptive. Rather than manifesting only in potentially dangerous behavior, the patient could be helped to use it prosocially. For instance, the patient could be helped to identify occupational choices or other social outlets that are in line with the schema (Freeman & Davison, 1997).

The fourth level is *schema camouflage*. Interventions at this level do not directly impact on the schema. Most treatment interventions, particularly within a short-term therapy, will be focused on schema modification and reinterpretation. With more impaired individuals, schematic camouflage will also be used. For example, a parasuicidal borderline personality disordered individual could be helped to make a non-suicide contract and call a help-line when a self-destruction schema is experienced (Freeman & Davison, 1997).

The third step is to develop a treatment strategy for accomplishing this goal. When schema restructuring or modification is the goal, an important part of this strategy involves educating patients as to how their maladaptive schemas arose and are maintained. The schema restructuring and modification change process usually also involves a "life review." While constructing the life review, the patient provides evidence that supports the schema as well as evidence that contradicts it. These schemas are tested through predictive experiments, guided observation, and reenactment of early schema-related incidents. A variety of emotive, interpersonal, behavioral, and cognitive techniques are used. Young (1994) detailed these schema reconstruction change interventions in his book, *Cognitive Therapy for Personality Disorder: A Schema-Focused Approach*.

Through the cognitive analysis of life evidence, patients become able to distance themselves, rather than being overidentified with and controlled by the "voice" of the schemas. Only then can schemas be viewed as something they've learned through repeated indoctrination by early caregivers, siblings, and peers rather than as something inherent in themselves. Finally, these patients become more able to notice and remember counterschema data about themselves and their social experiences (Bricker, Young, & Flanagan, 1993).

☐ Description of Common Maladaptive Schemas

A promising development in Cognitive Therapy is Schema-Focused Cognitive Therapy (Bricker, Young, & Flanagan, 1993; Young, 1994). Fifteen maladaptive schema have been articulated based on clinical experience and research on the Schema Questionaire. Each of these schemas is briefly described.

Abandonment/Instability

The essential feature of this schema is the belief that significant others will not or cannot provide ongoing nurture, emotional support, strength, or protection because they are emotionally unstable and unreliable, or because they might die or abandon the patient in favor of someone else. This schema develops because of parental inconsistency in meeting the child's emotional needs. Parental separation, divorce, or other experiences of loss or abandonment such as illness or deaths of close relatives or peers can influence the internalization of this schema. Finally, individuals with this schema typically cling to relationships because of their exaggerated fears of being left alone or abandoned.

Abuse/Mistrust

The essential feature of this schema is the belief that others will hurt, abuse, humiliate, manipulate, or take advantage of one. The fear of others' violent outbursts can also be part of this schema. Others' negative behaviors are perceived as intentional or the result of extreme and unjustifiable negligence. This schema develops as a result of early childhood experiences of abuse from parents or siblings: physical, emotional, or sexual. Finally, individuals with this schema tend to be hypervigilant and accusatory of others' motives.

Emotional Deprivation

The essential feature of this schema involves the core belief that one's desire for a normal degree of emotional support will not be met by others. Individuals who have internalized this schema tend to feel deprived of nurturance, protection, or empathy. Deprivation of nurturance involves an absence of attention, affection, and warmth from others. Absence of strength, direction, or guidance from significant others leads to deprivation of protection. In the absence of understanding, listening, self-disclosure, or mutual sharing of feelings and experiences with others, these individuals experience deprivation of empathy. These individuals have usually experienced some emotional neglect in early childhood. They may present as cold, demanding, or withholding, and tend to choose significant others who are unwilling or unable to provide emotional support.

Functional Dependence/Incompetence

The essential feature of this schema involves the core belief of being unable to handle everyday responsibilities competently or without considerable help from others. Such everyday responsibilities include minor decisions, hassles, chores, and tasks that constitute an average day. The schema develops when parents fail to encourage or allow a sense of independence, self-sufficiency, or competence in the child. Consequently, they ask for help and reassurance in what they do, while making wrong decisions or exercising bad judgment when they are expected to function independently. Not surprisingly, they choose significant others on whom they can be dependent.

Vulnerability to Harm and Illness

The essential feature of this schema involves an exaggerated fear that major disaster will strike at any time and that one is unable to protect oneself from disaster. These disasters can include financial, medical, criminal, or natural catastrophic events. This schema develops in the context of overly protective parents who continually communicate that the world is dangerous and life is unpredictable. Accordingly, these individuals present with a host of unrealistic fears and are frequently diagnosed with anxiety disorders.

Enmeshment/Undeveloped Self

The essential feature of this schema is the core belief that excessive emotional closeness and involvement with significant others can only occur at the expense of full individuation and normal social development. This schema often involves the belief that the enmeshed individual cannot survive or be happy without the constant support or presence of the other. Enmeshed individuals often feel that they are fused with the other. As such they find it difficult to experience a sense of individual identity or inner direction. They will feel smothered when around the enmeshed other but will feel emptiness or panic when left alone. This schema develops within the context of an enmeshed family. Subsequently, these individuals find it extremely difficult to individuate and functionally separate from that family or enmeshing others.

Defectiveness/Shame

The essential feature of this schema involves the core belief that one is inwardly defective or flawed. As a result, these individuals believe they must be fundamentally unlovable or unacceptable. Consequently, they experience a deep sense of shame concerning their perceived inadequacies and constantly fear exposure and further rejection by significant others. This schema tends to develop in the context of constant criticism, devaluation, or rejection by parents. Subsequently, these individuals are hypersensitive and expect blame and rejection from others. They tend to be self-critical and exaggerate their own defects, while avoiding situations requiring self-disclosure and the risks associated with intimacy.

Social Undesirability/Alienation

The essential feature of this schema is the core belief that one is outwardly undesirable to, or different from, others. Individuals with this schema tend to belief that they are ugly, sexually undesirable, socially inept, or low in status. They feel self-conscious and insecure in social situations and subsequently become alienated or isolated from others. Therefore, they are likely to conclude that they are not part of any group or community. This schema usually develops in the context of repeated criticism of one's appearance, social behavior, or being treated differently than others. Subsequently, these individuals tend to feel more comfortable when alone because social circumstances trigger self-consciousness or pressure to pretend they are enjoying themselves.

Failure to Achieve

The essential feature of this schema is the belief that one will inevitably fail or that one's capacity to achieve is inferior to one's peers. Corollary

beliefs include the perception that one is inadequate, untalented, or igno-
rant. This schema tends to develop in the context of parental criticism
usually involving invidious comparisons with siblings or peers. It can also
arise when parents fail to provide sufficient encouragement, direction, or
support. Subsequently, these individuals perceive they have failed in comparison to others even when their performance meets or exceeds that of
others.

Subjugation

The essential feature of this schema is the surrender of control over one's
own decisions and preferences to others. The purpose of this self-surren-
der is to avoid anger, retaliation, or abandonment. Subjugated individuals
perceive their desires are neither valid nor important to others. Not surprisingly, this perception often leads to anger at those who subjugate. This
schema usually develops in the context of domineering or controlling parents who punish, threaten, or withdraw from the child for expressing needs
or wants. Subsequently, these individuals present as overly compliant or
underassertive who avoid conflict and confrontation at all cost.

Self-Sacrifice/Overresponsibility

The essential feature of this schema involves a voluntary but excessive
focus on meeting the needs of others at the expense of one's own needs.
Such self-sacrifice and overresponsibility is motivated by a desire to spare
others pain, to maintain a connection with others who are perceived as
more needy, to avoid guilt, or to gain self-esteem. While self-sacrifice results from sensitivity to the pain of others, it often leads to a feeling that
one's own needs are not being met and to resentment of those for whom
one sacrifices. This schema tends to develop in the context of an emotionally needy parent who expects or requires the child to assume a caretaker
role at a very early age. Guilt is a prominent feature of this schema. Subsequently, these individuals place the needs of others before their own and
tend to overextend and over commit themselves.

Emotional Inhibition

The essential feature of this schema involves excessive inhibition of emotions and impulses. These individuals anticipate that the expression of

emotions and impulses will invariably result in loss of self-esteem, embarrassment, abandonment, or harm to self or others. This schema develops in the context of parents who promote the value of emotional control and discourage the expression of affect, particularly anger. Subsequently, these individuals appear cold and nonspontaneous and are also quite uncomfortable around displays of positive affect. Not surprisingly, they tend to choose significant others who are also controlled and rigid, or who are highly emotive so they can vicariously experience some emotional freedom.

Unrelenting/Unbalanced Standards

The essential feature of this schema is the relentless striving to meet the high flown expectations of oneself at the expense of happiness, spontaneity, health, and satisfying interpersonal relationships. It often includes unrealistic expectations of others. Individuals who have internalized this schema place undue emphasis on following strict personal rules of behavior or morality, and ignore their basic needs for gratification and enjoyment. They may also value status, money, achievement, or recognition over inner peace and harmony. This schema tends to develop in the context of parents with extremely high standards of achievement or moral superiority, and who make their love and approval dependent on task accomplishment. Subsequently, these individuals may be quite accomplished and successful, but also suffer from anxiety, depression, or stress-related complaints or disorders. Not surprisingly, these individuals tend to choose significant others who will also be highly critical of them or whom they can criticize and demand perfection.

Entitlement/Self-Centeredness

The essential feature of this schema is the belief that one is entitled to whatever one wants irrespective of the cost to others or of what might be regarded as unreasonable. This schema is likely to develop in the context of parents who overindulge or who do not encourage the child to develop self-responsibility. Alternatively, this schema can develop as a compensation for feelings of deprivation, social undesirability, or defectiveness. Subsequently, individuals who develop this schema tend to be self-centered and have an exaggerated view of themselves and their rights. They also tend to have significant empathic deficits and tend to treat others carelessly.

Insufficient Self-Control/Self-Discipline

The essential feature of this schema is the belief that it is extremely difficult to exercise sufficient self-control or frustration tolerance in the process of achieving personal goals or refraining from impulsive behaviors or emotional outbursts. This schema tends to develop in the context of parents who failed to model self-control, to set limits, or to adequately discipline the child. Alternatively, the schema can develop as a result of intolerable feelings of insecurity or tension arising from an unstable home environment. Subsequently, these individuals exhibit problems of impulsivity and aggressivity and have considerable difficulty delaying gratification.

☐ Summary

Traditionally, character, which is conceptualized as the learned, psychosocial component of personality, has been the focus of psychodynamically oriented psychotherapies. Today, the term *schema* is being used to operationalize the characterological component of personality. Although the construct of schema is used by both psychodynamic clinicians and cognitive therapy clinicians, it is the schema-focused approach to cognitive therapy that has developed a systematic approach to the treatment of the personality disorders. In this approach, the clinician works collaboratively with the patient to assess and then modify maladaptive schemas. This chapter has described 15 maladaptive schemas that are commonly observed in personality disordered individuals.

Temperament and Style Change

Temperament refers to the innate, genetic, and constitutional influences on personality. Whereas character and schema reflect the psychological dimension of personality, temperament reflects the biological dimension of personality. This chapter describes the dimensions of temperament in terms of its regulation and dysregulation of behavior. It then briefly provides an overview of skills, skill deficits, and skill training and their role in regulating or modulating the temperament/style dimensions of personality disordered individuals. Finally, 15 intervention strategies useful in this modulation process are described. At least one resource citation is provided for each strategy. Reference is made to these strategies in other chapters of this book.

Cloninger (1993) contended that temperament has four biological dimensions—novelty seeking, harm avoidance, reward dependence, and persistence—whereas character has three quantifiable dimensions: self-directedness or self-responsibility, cooperativeness, and self-transcendence. Other researchers would describe impulsivity and aggressivity as additional dimensions of temperament (Costello, 1996). Harm avoidance or behavioral inhibition can be thought of as inhibition of behavior in response to a stimuli. Thus, the more easily and intensely upset a person is by noxious stimuli, the more likely the person is to avoid it. Reward dependence or behavioral maintenance refers to the ease or difficulty with which a person becomes hooked on pleasurable behavior and the degree to the behavior remains controlled by it. Finally, novelty seeking or behavioral activation is the heritable tendency toward exhilaration in response to novel stimuli or cues that have previously been associated with pleasure or relief of discomfort. In other words, it involves the activation of behavior in response to potentially pleasurable stimuli. Each of these temperament dimensions is putatively related to a neurotransmitter system: dopamine to behavioral activation, serotonin to behavioral inhibition, and norepinephrine to behavioral maintenance (Cloninger, 1993). As noted in Chapter 1, the influence of temperament is reflected in the individual's basic styles: affective style, behavioral/relational style, and cognitive style.

Cloninger noted that temperament and character can be measured with biological markers and self-report instruments. On Temperament Character Inventory (TCI), individuals with increased dysregulation of one or more of the temperament dimensions typically experience considerable distress and impairment in life functioning. For example, according to Cloninger's research (1993) the borderline personality disorder would likely rate as high in novelty seeking and harm avoidance, low in reward dependence, while also rating low on three character dimensions. Just as schema—and its modification—is central to this book, so also is temperament and style—and its modulation.

☐   Skills, Skill Deficits, and Skills Training

Effective functioning in daily life requires mastery of a number of requisite personal and relational skills. Most individuals begin learning these requisite skills in childhood and further refine them throughout the course of adolescence and early adulthood. Some patients have the requisite skills but for conscious or unconscious reasons do not use them. Other patients have never learned or sufficiently mastered these skills. This lack of learning or mastery of a basic requisite skill is called a skill deficit (Lieberman, DeRisi, & Mueser, 1989). It is a basic premise of this book that most personality disordered individuals have skill deficits. Because of these deficits, these individuals experience, to varying degrees, dysregulation of one or more temperament dimensions that cause distress to themselves or others. The three temperament or style dimensions emphasized in this book are affective style, behavioral and relational style, and cognitive style. Over- or undermodulation of one or more of these styles can significantly affect level of symptoms and level of functioning (i.e., GAF). In other words, requisite skills—including coping skills—have the effect of regulating or modulating temperament or style dimensions, whereas skill deficits make it more difficult, if not impossible, to modulate style dimensions.

Recall the case examples in Chapter 1. Both Keri and Cindy presented for treatment following a suicide gesture. Although both had the same diagnosis and level of education, Keri's GAF was 40 (with 71 as the highest in the past year) and Cindy's was 27 (with 42 as the highest in the past year). Keri's high level of premorbid functioning suggested that she had mastered most requisite skills, including coping skills, to achieve her level of success. Cindy, on the other hand, had significant skill deficits, which explains why affective, behavioral/relational, and cognitive styles were so overmodulated.

Clinicians can effectively assist patients in reversing such skill deficits by working with them to acquire the personal and relational skills that they have not previously mastered. These skills can be learned directly in individual sessions through practice, that is, coaching and role playing, and through graded task assignment. When feasible, group treatment settings can be particularly useful for social skills training (Lieberman et al., 1989).

For those personality disordered patients with significant symptomatic distress and who exhibit significant functional impairment, traditional psychotherapeutic interventions are of limited use. However, medication and structured interventions—called *skills training*—are quite effective when temperament dysregulation is present. In addition, these structured interventions are effective when skill deficits and reversing these deficits are indicated.

☐ Structured Treatment Interventions for Personality Disorders

The 15 structured interventions are detailed in Table 3.1. These interventions have been referred to throughout the book. Each intervention is described in a step-wise fashion that illustrates its application in the treatment setting. At least one key reference or resource is provided for each of these interventions so that the reader may pursue additional information on using these effective therapeutic interventions.

Anger Management Training

The purpose of anger management training is to decrease the arousal and expression of hostile affects, while increasing the individual's capacity to tolerate and channel this energy in prosocial ways. This is usually a thera-

---

TABLE 3.1. Structured Intervention Strategies for Personality Disorders

---

1. Anger Management
2. Anxiety Management Training
3. Assertiveness Training
4. Cognitive Awareness Training
5. Distress Tolerance Training
6. Emotional Regulation Training
7. Limit Setting
8. Empathy Training
9. Impulse Control Training
10. Interpersonal Skills Training
11. Problem Solving Training
12. Self-Management Training
13. Sensitivity Reduction Training
14. Symptom Management Training
15. Thought Stopping

---

pist-directed intervention that can be applied in individual- or group-treatment context. It is then practiced and applied by the individual. Collaboration between clinician and the individual tends to increase the individual's motivation and compliance. The intervention proceeds in the following fashion.

First, the clinician instructs the patient in the four sets of factors that determine the response of anger in that patient: (a) high-risk circumstances (external, contextual factors, such as individuals, places, or times of day that can potentially provoke an angry or rageful response in the patient); (b) internal triggering factors (internal factors, such as the patient's feelings, cravings, level of fatigue that render the patient more vulnerable to an angry response); (c) patient self-statements (specific beliefs that can render the patient more vulnerable to an angry response, or that can defuse an angry response); and (d) patient's coping skills that neutralize or exacerbate the effects of these internal and external factors.

Second, the clinician instructs/trains the patient in identifying the four sets of factors, and develops—with the patient—a checklist or form of the most likely factors for that patient. For example, the clinician asks the patient to describe a recent instance of a response of anger, and assists the patient in indicating the four specific factors. He had gotten stopped for speeding and for driving while under the influence of alcohol: (a) he left a tavern after four drinks and decided to drive home rather than take a cab (high-risk circumstance); (b) he was tired after a stressful day at work and was disinhibited and feeling bad that someone had just broken his car aerial (internal triggering factor); (c) he was thinking: "Why does this stuff always happen to me?" and "Nobody does this to my car and gets away with it" (self-statement); and (d)he is impulsive with a "hair-trigger" temper (coping skills) and speeds off angry and resentful.

Third, the clinician tells the patient to write down each incident in which he felt anger, the four factors, and what he did when he experienced that emotion (i.e., cursed and kicked the side of his car when he noticed the car aerial was broken). The patient then self-monitors these factors and responses between sessions with the form. During subsequent sessions, the clinician and patient review the form. They analyze the factors looking for commonalities and specifying coping skill deficits (i.e., he's mostly likely to be angry and disinhibited when he's tired, been stressed at work, or been drinking).

Fourth, the clinician works with the patient to specify alternatives to these high-risk circumstances (i.e., if he's been drinking he'll take a cab or ask a designated driver to get home). Then, the clinician helps the patient to specify a plan for reducing the various internal triggering factors (i.e., when he's tired and stressed out he can go jogging rather than go to the tavern).

Fifth, the clinician instructs and assists the patient to learn effective, alternative self-statements to cope with anger-provocation (i.e., "It's too bad this happened, but I don't have to go ballistic over it").

Finally, the clinician trains the patient in learning relaxation skills (i.e., controlled breathing and counting to 10 before acting when he sees that his car has been vandalized) and other coping skills such as assertive communication as an alternative to the anger and rageful responses.

Resources

Novaco, R. (1975). *Anger control*. Lexington, MA: Heath/Lexington Books.
Novaco, R. (1984). Stress inoculation therapy for anger control. In P. Keller & L. Ritt (Eds.), *Innovations in clinical practice: A source book* (pp. 214–222). Sarasota, FL: Professional Resource Exchange.

Anxiety Management Training

The purpose of anxiety management training is to decrease the arousal and expression of distressing affects, and to increase the individual's capacity to face and tolerate these affects. This is usually a therapist-directed intervention that can be applied in individual- or group-treatment context. It is then practiced and applied by the individual. Collaboration between clinician and the individual tends to increase the individual's motivation and compliance. The intervention proceeds in the following fashion.

First, the clinician instructs the patient in the determinants of the response of anxiety in that patient: (a) external triggering factors, such as specific individuals or stressful demands that can potentially elicit anxiety in the patient; (b) internal triggering factors, such as physiological responsivity and patient self-statements, that is, specific beliefs that can render the patient more vulnerable to anxiety, or that can neutralize it; and (c) patient's coping skills that neutralize or exacerbate the effects of these internal and external factors.

Second, the clinician instructs the patient in identifying the three sets of factors, and develops—with the patient—a checklist of the most likely factors for that patient. The clinician then asks the patient to describe a recent incidence of anxiety and assists the patient to specify the three specific factors. In the example of performance anxiety, the patient is (a) assigned to give a quarterly business report at a board of directors meeting (external trigger); (b) experienced moderate physiological reactivity during other public presentations: "I feel completely inadequate giving a speech to my superiors." "I know I'm going to screw up, and I'll be so embarrassed" [internal triggers]; and (c) prefaces the presentation by asking the group's indulgence saying she is a better accountant than public speaker (coping skills) and experiences feelings of inadequacy, dry mouth, sweaty palms and heart palpitations while giving the presentation. Alternately, an anxiety survey can be used, and if there are more than one anxiety responses, an anxiety hierarchy survey can be used.

Third, the clinician tells the patient to write down each incident in which she has experienced anxiety, the three factors, and what she did when experiencing that emotion (i.e., she quickly excused herself after giving the report, experienced some relief, but concluded she had failed again). The patient then self-monitors these factors and responses between sessions with the form.

Fourth, during subsequent sessions the clinician and patient review the checklist. They analyze the factors looking for commonalities and specifying coping skill deficit (i.e., she's likely to experience performance anxiety when addressing superiors, although she has no problem giving presentations to peers or inferiors).

Fifth, the clinician works with the patient to consider options when faced with external triggers (i.e., to inquire about submitting a written rather than verbal report, or having a colleague give the presentation, while she is present to field questions on the report).

Sixth, the clinician works with the patient to specify a plan for reducing the various internal triggering factors, that is, learning to reduce physiological reactivity by controlled breathing or other relaxation exercises, and specifying more adaptive self-statements, that is, "My worth as a person and as an employee doesn't dependent on how well I can give speeches. This is only one small part of my job"; "I know this material cold—certainly better than anyone on board. I can get through this 5-minute talk and maybe even enjoy it."

Seventh, the clinician trains the patient in learning relaxation skills, such as controlled breathing 10 minutes prior to giving a presentation, and other coping skills as an alternative to the anxiety and self-deprecatory responses. Treatment progress is evaluated based on the patient's increasing capacity to face internal and external triggering factors with more adaptive coping behaviors. The patient's self-report of the absence of, or a significant reduction in, anxiety in such circumstances indicates the treatment has been effective.

Resources

Suinn, R. (1977). *Manual: Anxiety management training*. CO: Rocky Mountain Behavioral Science Institute.

Suinn, R., & Deffenbacher, J. (1982). The self-control of anxiety. In P. Karoly & F. Kanfer (Eds.), *The psychology of self-management: From theory to practice* (pp. 132–141). New York: Pergamon.

Assertiveness Training

The purpose of assertiveness training is to increase an individual's capacity for expressing thoughts, feelings, and beliefs in a direct, honest, and appropriate manner without violating the rights of others. More specifically, it involves the capacity to say "no," to make requests, to express positive and negative feelings, and to initiate, continue, and terminate conversations. Lack of assertive behavior is usually related to specific skills deficits, but it is sometimes related to interfering emotional reactions and thoughts. Assertiveness training proceeds in the following fashion.

First, the clinician performs a careful assessment to identify the following: situations of concern to the patient; current assertiveness skills; personal and environmental obstacles that need to be addressed, such as difficult significant others or limited social contexts; and personal and environmental resources that can be drawn on.

Second, the clinician formulates an intervention plan. If appropriate behaviors are available but not performed because of anxiety, the focus may be on enhancing anxiety management skills. Discrimination training is required when skills are available but are not performed at appropriate times. If skill deficits are present, skill training is indicated.

Third, the intervention is introduced. For skill training, the clinician teaches the patient specific skills via modeling, behavioral rehearsal, feedback, and homework. Modeling effective behavior in specific situations is accomplished by using one or more of the following methods: in vivo demonstration of the behavior by the clinician, written scripts, videotapes, audiotapes, or films. In behavior rehearsal, the patient is provided opportunities to practice the given skill in the clinical setting.

Fourth, the clinician provides positive feedback following each rehearsal in which effective verbal and nonverbal reactions are noted and specific changes that could be made to enhance performance are identified. Homework assignments involve tasks that the patient agrees to carry out in real-life contexts.

Fifth, the length of assertion training depends on the domain of social behaviors that must be developed and on the severity of countervailing personal and environmental obstacles. If the response repertoire is narrow, such as refusing requests, and the obstacles minor, only a few sessions may be required. If the behavior deficits are extensive, additional time may be required even though only one or two kinds of social situations are focused on during intervention. Assertiveness training can occur in individual sessions, group therapy, as well as in other small contexts such as support groups and workshops. Sank and Shaffer (1984) provided a detailed four-session assertiveness training module for use in a structured group therapy context.

Resources

Alberti, R. (1978). *Assertiveness: Applications and issues*. San Luis Obispo, CA: Impact Publications.

Sank, L. & Shaffer, C. (1984). *A therapist's manual for cognitive behavior therapy in groups*. New York: Plenum.

Cognitive Awareness Training

The purpose of cognitive awareness training is to reduce narcissistic injury, projective identification, and cognitive distortions. Increased recognition and awareness of distorted thinking and unrealistic expectations can attenuate resulting distress and acting out behaviors. As such, this intervention is particularly useful in the treatment of personality disordered individuals. Although this intervention is clinician-initiated, it is essentially a self-management intervention that the individual must practice sufficiently to achieve some level of mastery. The intervention proceeds in the following fashion.

First, the clinician assesses the nature of the patient's cognitive distress, because the intervention is applied somewhat differently for narcissistic injury and projective identification than it is for cognitive distortions.

Second, assuming that the distress is attributed to narcissistic injury or projective identification, the clinician focuses cognitive awareness training on the social interactions that trigger dysfunctional conflicts. The goal is to understand the relationship between the other's anger-provoking behavior and the individual's own frustrated expectations. This involves specifying what it was about the other's behavior that was frustrating or hurtful, and identifying what expectations were frustrated by the other's behavior. In using this technique, it is essential that the clinician help the individual to distinguish the reasonable aspects of the individual's expectations from the unreasonable aspect(s). Failure to recognize this expectation will be experienced by the individual as a narcissistic injury.

Third, assuming that the distress is attributed to cognitive distortion, the clinician focuses cognitive awareness training on the patient's thoughts and images associated with the onset and escalation of conflict. The clinician inquires about the individual's inner experience when anger begins welling up: What were their thoughts, self-talk, and images of the other person as the argument began to escalate? By monitoring these cognitions, the individual can bring into conscious awareness many irrational thoughts and perceptions that had previously been either out of awareness or vague.

Resource

Novaco, R. (1978). Anger and coping with stress: Cognitive behavioral interventions. In J. Foreyth & D. Rathjen (Eds.), *Cognitive behavior therapy* (pp. 217–243). New York: Plenum.

Distress Tolerance Skill Training

Distress tolerance is the capacity to perceive one's environment without demanding it be different, to experience one's current emotional state without attempting to change it, and to observe one's thought and action patterns without attempting to stop them. Thus, it is the ability to tolerate difficult situations and accept them. Typically, lower functioning individuals with borderline and histrionic personality disorders have difficulty tolerating distress. Distress tolerance training attempts to help the patient to develop skills and strategies to tolerate and survive crises and to accept life as it is in the moment. Among individuals with mood lability and impulsivity, the ability to tolerate distress is a prerequisite for other therapeutic change. This intervention is usually introduced and demonstrated by the clinician. It is then practiced and applied by the individual. As such, it is a self-management intervention. Initially, the clinician may have to cue the individual to apply the technique within and between treatment sessions. The intervention proceeds in the following fashion.

First, the clinician assesses the patient's ability to distract themselves from painful emotional thoughts and feelings, and to soothe themselves in the face of worry, loneliness, and distress. Skill deficits in either or both areas are noted.

Second, based on this assessment, the clinician instructs the patient in one or both of the following essential skills and strategies: distraction and self-soothing methods. If distraction is a basic skill deficit, it becomes the focus of treatment. Distraction techniques include thought stopping, shifting attention by making a phone call, watching television or listening to music, jogging, comparing oneself to others who are less well off, and intense sensations; for example, placing one's hand in a container of ice water or flicking a thick rubber band on one's wrist to produce a painful but harmless sensation intense enough to derail the thought and impulse for wrist-cutting and other self-harmful behaviors.

Third, if self-soothing is a basic skill deficit, it becomes the focus of treatment. Self-soothing techniques include controlled breathing exercises—in which air is drawn in slowly and deeply and then exhaled slowly and completely—savoring a favorite food or snack, and listening to or humming a soothing melody. Acceptance skills include radical acceptance—complete acceptance from deep within, turning the mind toward acceptance—choosing to accept reality as it is, and willingness versus willfulness.

Resources

Linehan, M. (1993a). *Cognitive-behavioral treatment of borderline personality disorder*. New York: Guilford.
Linehan, M. (1993b). *Skill training manual for treating borderline personality disorder*. New York: Guilford.

Emotion Regulation Skill Training

Patients who habitually exhibit emotional lability may benefit from help in learning to regulate their emotions. Emotion regulation skills can be extremely difficult to teach, because emotionally labile patients often believe that if they could only "change their attitude" they could change their feelings. Labile patients often come from environments where others exhibits cognitive control of their emotions, and show little tolerance of the patients' inability to exhibit similar control. Subsequently, labile patients often resist attempts to control their emotions because such control implies that others are right and they are wrong for feeling the way they do. Much of the labile patient's emotional distress is a result of such secondary responses as intense shame, anxiety, or rage to primary emotions. Often the primary emotions are adaptive and appropriate to the context. The reduction of this secondary distress requires exposure to the primary emotions in a nonjudgmental atmosphere. Accordingly, mindfulness to one's own emotional responses is essentially an exposure technique. This intervention typically proceeds in the following fashion.

First, the clinician assesses the patient's overall skill in emotional regulation, and then the subskills of identifying and labeling affects, modulating affects, and mindfulness.

Second, the clinician formulates a plan for reversing the skill deficit(s). Skill training can occur in either an individual- or group-treatment context. Although the skills of emotion regulation can be learned in an individual-treatment context, group context greatly facilitates these efforts. Skill training groups can provide a measure of social support and peer feedback that individual treatment cannot.

Third, the clinician, whether in an individual- or a skill-group context, teaches, models, and coaches the patient(s) in the given subskill of emotional regulation. The first step in regulating emotions is learning to identify and label emotions. Identification of an emotional response involves the ability to observe one's own responses as well as to describe accurately the context in which the emotions occur. Identification is greatly aided if one can observe and describe the event prompting the emotion, can interpret the event that prompts the emotion, can differentiate the phenomonological experience, including physical sensations of the emotion, and can describe its effects on one's own functioning.

Similarly, emotional lability can be attenuated by controlling the events that trigger emotions or by reducing the individual's vulnerability to lability. Patients are more susceptible to emotional lability when they are under physical or environmental stress. Accordingly, patients should be assisted in reducing such stressors by achieving a more balanced lifestyle. This includes appropriate nutrition, sufficient sleep, adequate exercise, reduction of substance use, and increased self-efficacy. Although these targets seem straightforward, making headway on them with labile patients can be exhausting for both patients and clinicians. Work on any of these targets requires an active stance by the patients and persistence until positive effects begin to accrue.

Increasing the number of positive events in one's life is one approach to increasing positive emotions. Initially, this involves increasing daily positive experiences. Subsequently, it means making life changes so that positive events will occur more often.

In addition to increasing positive events, it is also useful to work on being mindful of positive experiences when they occur, and unmindful of worries that the positive experience will end. Mindfulness to current emotions means experiencing emotions without judging them or trying to inhibit them, block them, or distract from them. The assumption is that exposure to painful or distressing emotions, without association to negative consequences, will extinguish their ability to stimulate secondary negative emotions. Whenever a patient already feels "bad," judging negative emotions as "bad" leads to feelings of guilt, anger, or anxiety, which further increases distress intolerance. Frequently, patients can tolerate a painful affect if they can refrain from feeling guilty or anxious about feeling bad in the first place.

Fourth, the clinician works together with the patient to arrange for the patient to practice a given skill(s) both within and outside the treatment context. Within the treatment context, the use of role play can be particularly valuable in reinforcing the patient's newly acquired skill(s). Particular situations and relationships can be targeted for practice outside the treatment context.

Resources

Linehan, M. (1993). *Cognitive-behavioral treatment of borderline personality disorder*. New York: Guilford.

Linehan, M. (1993). *Skill training manual for treating borderline personality disorder*. New York: Guilford.

Limit Setting

Limit setting is an intervention designed to help patients recognize aspects of themselves that are being defended against by resorting to a destructive, outer-directed activity or diversion. Personality disordered individuals often have difficulty maintaining boundaries, as well as appreciating and anticipating the consequences, especially the negative consequences, of their actions. Limit setting is a therapeutic intervention that is quite useful in as well as outside treatment settings. The intervention proceeds in the following fashion.

First, the clinician observes or anticipates one of the following patient behaviors: treatment-interfering behaviors, such as coming late for sessions, missing a session, unnecessarily delaying or failing to make payment; harmful behavior to self or others, including parasuicidal behaviors; inappropriate verbal behavior (e.g., abusive language); dominating treatment by excessive or rambling speech; efforts to communicate with the clinician outside the treatment context (i.e., unnecessary phone calls); inappropriate actions (e.g., hitting or unwanted touching, breaking or stealing items); or failure to complete assigned therapeutic tasks (i.e., homework). For example, a fashionably dressed patient complained of financial hardships and requested a special reduced fee and payment schedule.

Second, the clinician begins implementing limit setting. The clinician begins by setting the limit. The limit is specified in "if ___ then ___" language. It is crucial that the clinician state the limit in a neutral, non-critical tone and non-judgmental language. In the above example, rather than making special concessions to him, the standard fee arrangements were clearly explained. He was told that if he could not afford to be seen at the clinic, the clinician would be sorry but would assist him in finding lower cost treatment

Third, the clinician explains the rationale for the limit. In the above example, it was further explained that allowing him to accumulate a sizable bill would not be in his best interest.

Fourth, the clinician specifies or negotiates with the patient the consequences for breaching the limit. In the above example, that clinician told the patient that if he would fall behind in payments by two sessions, according to clinic policy, he would need to wait until his balance was current before additional sessions would be scheduled.

Fifth, the clinician responds to any breeches of the limit setting. Because patients can and do test limits—whether for conscious or unconscious reasons—more commonly in the early phase of treatment, limit testing should be expected. The clinician should be prepared to respond by confronting and/or interpreting it; enforcing the consequences and discussing the impact of the breech on treatment; or predicting that such testing may reoccur. For example, in the above case, the patient did test the agreement once; the clinician expressed concern but upheld the limit. Thereafter, the patient kept up with his payments and his treatment continued.

Resource

Green, S. (1988). *Limit setting in clinical practice*. Washington, DC: American Psychiatric Press.

Empathy Training

Empathy training is a technique for more directly enhancing the patient's empathic abilities. In empathy training, the patient is asked to think about and then communicate his/her understanding of the feelings and point of view of the other. These understandings are then checked out with the other individual and inaccuracies are corrected. Particular attention is given to the patient's understanding of what he/she has done or said that has aroused hurt feelings in the other, and what the other wishes would have happened instead of what did happen. The technique of empathy training is a powerful tool for interrupting projective identification and splitting. It often leads to greatly increased awareness of the feelings and needs of the other. This, in turn, greatly facilitates constructive negotiation and problem solving. Although there are various approaches to empathy training, the relationship enhancement approach has been demonstrated to be effective with personality disordered individuals, including individuals with narcissistic personality disorder in a relatively short time—three to four sessions—particularly if empathy training takes place in the context of couples sessions. The intervention proceeds in the following fashion.

First, the clinician assesses the nature and extent of the patient's capacity to manifest the three skills of empathy: active listening, accurately interpreting interpersonal cues, and responding empathically.

Second, assuming an empathic deficit (i.e., in one or more of the three skills of empathy), the clinician begins the training by modeling the three skills of empathy. After being continually modeled by the clinician, the patient begins to develop empathic understanding and responding.

Third, the clinician begins to coach the patient on the given skill(s) beginning with non-relationship issues, and then moving to positive feelings before progressing to conflicts. The clinician teaches the patient to access the underlying vulnerability and the healthy needs that underlie his narcissistic defense. This is done through the dual process of empathic listening and the coaching of skilled expression of one's authentic feelings and point of view. The patient initially tends both to experience and express vulnerability in the form of anger, criticism, and blame. Empathic listening becomes a way of calming the patient's reflexive reactions and of creating a pause between emotions and the reflexive, harmful behaviors that have resulted from those emotions.

Fourth, empathy training also assists patients in monitoring their emotional reactivity. Patients typically experience that listening empathically and responding within the guidelines for effective expression feels supportive to them. They also begin to discover that when emotions are accurately observed and expressed subjectively with increasing consciousness of how meanings affect feelings, these emotions shift or even vanish quite rapidly. What often perpetuates anger, for example, is the lack of full attention to it on the part of the patient, and to the meanings and desires it reveals. When this attention neither inhibits nor defends the emotion, but instead maintains a compassionate and curious observer stance, change in feelings, meanings, and actions can occur quickly.

Resources

Guerney, B. (1977). *Relationship enhancement: Skills programs for therapy, problem prevention, and enrichment.* San Francisco: Jossey-Bass.
Guerney, B. (1988). *Relationship enhancement manual.* State College, PA: IDEALS.

Impulse Control Training

Impulse control training is an intervention whose goal is to reduce involuntary urges to act. This intervention is usually introduced and demonstrated by the clinician. It is then practiced and applied by the individual. As a result of applying this intervention, the individual increases self-control. This intervention involves three phases: assessment, training, and application. The intervention proceeds in the following fashion.

First, the clinician undertakes an assessment of the pattern of the patient's thoughts and feelings that lead up to self-destructive or maladaptive impulsive behavior. Once this pattern is understood, it is possible for the patient to find other ways to accomplish the same result that have fewer negative effects and are more likely to be adaptive.

Second, the clinician and patient examine the patient's thoughts and feelings leading up to self-destructive or maladaptive impulse behaviors.

For example, the patient keeps a log of thoughts and feelings associated with each impulsive behavior.

Third, the clinician teaches the patient competing responses to impulses by inducing an urge to act impulsively, and then helping the patient to implement strategies to delay acting on that impulse for progressively longer periods of time, which can be cognitive (i.e., counting to 10 before acting or speaking when upset) or muscle relaxation (i.e., progressive relaxation). The most common competing responses are systematic distractions that are either internal or external. Internal distractions are thoughts that are incompatible with the impulses. For example, the patient's self-talk becomes: "This is actually funny, and I'm going to smile instead of fume." External distractions include a change in the environment that focuses the patient's attention. For instance, the patient is prompted to leave the room when a parent is shouting at him and in the past, he has the impulse to hit the parent.

Fourth, the clinician helps the patient practice and supplies feedback until the patient develops a reasonable level of mastery. The clinician teaches the patient to apply internal and/or external distractions to neutralize maladaptive impulses. For example, when the patient is around his father who is drinking, he avoids getting hooked into fighting by conjuring up an image of Charlie Chaplin walking with a drunken limp and telling his father he has to leave to meet a friend.

Finally, because self-destructive impulsive behavior can be particularly problematic, it is essential for the clinician to develop a clear understanding of a patient's motivation for self-destructive behavior by examining the thoughts and feelings leading up to the self-destructive impulses or behavior, and then by asking directly, "What were you trying to accomplish through this action?" Suicide attempts, self-mutilation, and other self-destructive acts can be the product of many different motives: desire to punish others at whom the client is angry, desire to punish oneself or obtain relief from guilt, desire to distract oneself from even more aversive obsessions, and so forth. Once the motivation is understood, it is possible for the patient to find other ways to accomplish the same result that have fewer untoward effects and are more likely to be adaptive. For example, it may be possible to substitute a minimally self-destructive behavior, such as marking oneself with a pen, for a more self-destructive act, such as wrist-slashing. This less destructive act can later be replaced with a more adaptive alternative. Not surprisingly, if the risk of the patient's performing seriously self-destructive acts is high, and the above-described interventions do not prove effective in the limited time available, hospitalization may be needed to allow sufficient time for effective intervention.

Resources

Linehan, M. (1993). *Skill training manual for treating borderline personality disorder*. New York: Guilford.

Turkat, I. (1990). *The personality disorders: A psychological approach to clinical management*. New York: Pergamon Press.

Interpersonal Skills Training

Interpersonal skills refer to a broad range of skills in relating socially and/or intimately with others. These include distress tolerance, emotional regulation, impulse control, active listening, assertiveness, problem solving, friendship skills, negotiation, and conflict resolution. Lower functioning personality disordered individuals may have significant skill deficits, while higher functioning personality disordered individuals tend to have better developed conversational skills. However, to be effective interpersonally requires much more than the capability of producing automatic responses to routine situations. It also requires skills in producing novel responses or a combination of responses when the situation demands. Interpersonal effectiveness is the capacity to appropriately respond assertively, to negotiate reasonably, and to cope effectively with interpersonal conflict. Effectiveness means obtaining the changes one wants, by keeping the relationship and one's self-respect. And, even if higher functioning borderline patients possess adequate interpersonal skills, problems arise in the application of these skills in difficult situations. They may be able to describe effective behavioral sequences when discussing another person encountering a problematic situation but may be totally unable of carrying out a similar behavioral sequence when analyzing their own situation. Usually, the problem is that both belief patterns and uncontrollable affective responses are inhibiting the application of social skills. These patients often prematurely terminate relationships, or their skill deficits in distress tolerance make it difficult to tolerate the fears, anxieties, or frustrations that are typical in conflictual situations. Similarly, problems in impulse control and emotional regulation lead to inability to decrease chronic anger or frustration. Furthermore, skill deficit problem-solving skills make it difficult to turn potential relationship conflicts into positive encounters. In short, interpersonal competence requires most of the other skills described in this chapter as well as others. The intervention proceeds in the following fashion.

First, the clinician must assess the patient's current relational skills and skill deficits. The skills to be assessed include distress tolerance, emotional regulation, impulse control, assertiveness, problem solving, active listening, friendship skills, negotiation, and conflict resolution. Specific skill deficits are noted.

Second, the clinician formulates a plan for dealing with the noted skill deficit(s). If there are global deficits, it might require referral to a group focused on social skills training. Such groups are invaluable in providing social support while patients are learning personal and interpersonal skills.

Third, skill training begins either in an individual- or group-treatment context. Usually the sequence involves modeling of a given skill, and then coaching to achieve increasing levels of mastery. Interventions that involve several modes of practice or enactment seem to be the most efficacious and time efficient. Video demonstration of the skills, role-play practice, and homework exercises are integral features of such an approach. Assuming that a patient who has been referred to a skills training group is also in individual treatment, the clinician assesses and monitors progress.

Fourth, the clinician works together with the patient to arrange for the patient to practice a given skill(s) outside the treatment context. This usually includes initiating conversations with strangers, making friends, making and going on dates. Assessment of the skill level is followed by additional modeling and coaching.

Resources

Liberman, R., De Risis, W., & Mueser, K. (1989). *Social skills training for psychiatric patients*. New York: Pergamon.

Linehan, M. (1993). *Cognitive-behavioral treatment of borderline personality disorder*. New York: Guilford.

Linehan, M. (1993). *Skill training manual for treating borderline personality disorder*. New York: Guilford.

Zimbardo, P. (1977). *Shyness*. New York: Jove.

Problem-Solving Skills Training

Problem-solving skills training is a treatment intervention strategy through which individuals learn to use an effective set of skills to cope with distressing or troublesome personal and interpersonal situations. The goals of this form of social skills training is to assist individuals in identifying problems that cause their distress, to teach them a systematic method of solving problems, and to equip them with a method for approaching future problems. Problem-solving training is often a brief method of intervention that can be used in individual-, couples-, and group-treatment contexts. This is a clinician-initiated intervention than requires some training and practice by the individual to master this set of skills. This intervention proceeds in the following fashion.

First, the clinician assesses the patient's capacity to solve problems in terms of the five skills involved in problem solving. The five are problem identification, goal setting, generating alternative courses of action, decision making, and implementation of the decided course of action.

Second, the clinician explores with the patient the origin and nature of a specific problematic situation (i.e., problem identification). For instance, the patient notes that she runs out of money about 1 week before receiving her monthly paycheck, because of impulse buying during the first 3 weeks of the month.

Third, the clinician helps the patient to assess the problem, identify causative factors, and set realistic goals. In the above example, impulse buying is identified as the cause, and the goal set is to budget money to last the entire month, and to save 10% in a bank account.

Fourth, the clinician helps the patient to generate alternative courses of action. In terms of the example, alternatives are discussed. One is to develop a 30-day budget, a second is to ask the employer for a biweekly paycheck, and the third is to have an automatic paycheck deposit to a bank account.

Fifth, the clinician helps the patient choose a course of action with regard to its short- and long-range consequences. In this example, the patient decides that setting up a budget is the most realistic short- and long-term course of action.

Sixth, the clinician offers information and supports the patient's efforts to implement the course of action. In this case, the patient agrees to meet with a financial planner and sets up a monthly and annual budget plan, and also opens a savings account.

Resource

Hawton, K., & Kirk, J. (1989). Problem-solving. In K. Hawton, P. Salkovskis, J. Kirk, & D. Clark (Eds.), *Cognitive behavior therapy for psychiatric problems*. Oxford, England: Oxford University Press.

Self-Management Skills

Self-management skills are needed to learn, maintain, and generalize new behaviors and to inhibit or extinguish undesirable behaviors and behavioral changes. In its widest sense, self-management means efforts to control, manage, or otherwise change one's own behavior, thoughts, or emotional responses to events. Thus, the skills of distress tolerance, emotion regulation, impulse control, and anger management can be thought of as self-management skills. More specifically, self-management skills refer to the behavior capabilities that an individual needs to acquire further skills. To the extent that patients are deficient in self-management skills, their ability to acquire other skills is seriously compromised. Patients often need some knowledge of the principles of behavior change to effectively learn self-management skills. For instance, a patient's belief that individuals change complex behavior patterns in a heroic show of willpower sets the stage for an accelerating cycle of failure and self-condemnation. The failure to master a goal becomes additional proof that explanations of failure, such as laziness, lack of motivation, or lack of willpower, are true. The clinician must confront and replace these notions of how individuals change. In short, principles of learning and behavioral control, as well as knowledge about how these principles apply in each individual's case, are important targets in teaching self-management skills. Learning these targeted concepts often involves changes in a patient's belief system. The intervention typically proceeds in the following manner.

First, the clinician assesses the patient's overall level of self-management, as well as specific subskills of goal setting, self-monitoring, environmental control, toleration of limited progress, and relapse prevention, noting skill deficit(s).

Second, the clinician formulates a plan for dealing with the noted skill deficit(s). If there are global deficits, it might require referral to a group focused on social skills training. Such groups are invaluable in providing social support while patients are learning personal and interpersonal skills.

Third, skill training begins either in an individual- or group-treatment context. Usually the sequence involves modeling of a given skill, and then coaching to achieve increasing levels of mastery. Interventions that involve several modes of practice or enactment seem to be the most efficacious and time efficient. Video demonstration of the skills, role-play practice, and homework exercises are integral features of such an approach. Assuming that a patient who has been referred to a skills training group is also in individual treatment, the clinician assesses and monitors progress.

Patients need to learn how to formulate positive goals in place of negative goals, to assess both positive and negative goals realistically, and to examine their life patterns from the point of view of values clarification. Patients typically believe that nothing short of perfection is an acceptable outcome. Behavior change goals are often sweeping in context and clearly exceed the skills the patients may possess. Clinicians will need to teach patients such skills as self-monitoring and environmental monitoring, setting up and evaluating baselines, and evaluating empirical data to determine relationships between antecedent and consequent events and their own responses. These skills are very similar to the hypothesis-testing skills taught in cognitive therapy.

The belief that a patient can overcome any set of environmental stimuli is based on the assumption that it is possible to function independently of one's environments. Given this belief, it is not surprising that some patients have skill deficits when it comes to using their environments as a means of controlling their own behavior. Nevertheless, some patients are more responsive to transitory environmental cues than others. As a result, the capability to manage environmental surroundings effectively can be particularly crucial. Techniques such as stimulus narrowing, that is, reducing the number of distracting events in the immediate environment, and stimulus avoidance, that is, avoiding events that trigger problematic behaviors, can be targeted to counteract the belief that willpower alone is sufficient.

Some patients respond to a relapse or small failure as an indication that they are total failures and may as well give up. Accordingly, they will develop a self-management plan and then unrealistically expect perfection in adhering to the plan. The issue and focus of relapse prevention is attitude change. It then becomes essential to teach patients to plan realistically for relapse, to develop strategies for accepting the possibility of a slip, and to ameliorate the negative effects of relapse.

Because some patients have limited tolerance for feeling bad, they have difficulties carrying out behavior change action plans that require perseverance. Rather, they will often seek a quick fix that involves setting unreasonably short time limits for relatively complex changes. In other words, they expect instantaneous progress. If it does not occur, they believe they have failed. Therefore, emphasizing the gradual nature of behavior change and tolerance of concomitant negative affect should be a major focus of clinician effort.

Fourth, the clinician works together with the patient to arrange for the patient to practice a given skill or skills outside the treatment context. This usually includes initiating conversations with strangers, making friends, making and going on dates. Assessment of the skill level is followed by additional modeling and coaching.

Resources

Linehan, M. (1993). *Cognitive-behavioral treatment of borderline personality disorder*. New York: Guilford.

Linehan, M. (1993). *Skill training manual for treating borderline personality disorder*. New York: Guilford.

Sensitivity Reduction Training

Sensitivity reduction training is an intervention to neutralize and delimit an individual's vulnerability to criticism, misperception, and suspiciousness. Individuals who habitually misperceive and negatively distort social cues are prone to defensive and acting out behaviors. Instead, this intervention teaches individuals to more accurately attend to, process, and respond more effectively to social cues. This is a clinician-initiated intervention wherein the clinician collaborates with the individual to learn and practice more accurate use of social information. This intervention proceeds in the following fashion.

First, the clinician recognizes that these oversensitivity reactions involve errors and distortions in the course of the information processing. Information processing can be thought of in terms of four components: attending, information processing, responding, and feedback. Subsequently, this intervention is directed to these four components.

Second, the clinician assesses how the individual attends to the full range of social cues. This can be done by reviewing important social interactions of the individual, and critically assessing how the individual attends to pertinent social cues. For instance, an individual reports that as he enters a social gathering, a small group of people look at him and smile, then he hears a whispered comment after which everyone laughs. If the individual selectively attends only to the whispered comment and disregards the other two cues: smiling and laughter, he could misperceive the situation and respond defensively. If the individual is not identifying and attending to such pertinent cues, the clinician focuses training in this area.

Third, the clinician then assesses the accuracy of the individual's interpretation of this social information. Selective attention and misperception can be processed as threatening. Teaching the individual to interpret social cues more accurately is essential. This training can be accomplished with role playing, videotaped feedback, and instruction.

Fourth, the clinician assesses how the patient responds to these cues. Responding refers to the individual's response to the social cues of others ranging spoken words, paralanguage, and overt actions. Responses can range from appropriate and prosocial to inappropriate and harmful. To the extent that the individual is able to accurately attend to and process social cues, the individual is more likely to appropriately respond to the cue. Training is directed at appropriate responding. Although the focus of training is often on verbal responding, at times the individual's tone of voice, facial expression, or hand gesturing needs to be changed to make it less menacing.

Fifth, the clinician assesses how the patient uses the consequences of his or her social behavior, and the extent to which it is appropriate or maladaptive. Negative feedback can be useful information and the individual needs to learn to use it constructively. Furthermore, with improvement in social behavior, positive consequences should accrue to the individual.

Resource

Turkat, I. (1990). *The personality disorders: A psychological approach to clinical management*. New York: Pergamon Press.

Symptom Management Training

Symptom management training is an intervention strategy for controlling the distressing manifestations (i.e., symptoms) of psychiatric disorders. Although symptoms are of varying types and levels of intensity and duration, patients tend to report symptoms without such differentiation, and unless the clinician clarifies the type and intensity/duration, referrals or needless changes in treatments, such as medication dosage or other medications added, can result in significant untoward effects on the treatment process. Personality disordered patients are more likely to experience low-grade, subclinical symptoms (i.e., persistent symptoms) than acute symptoms. Yet, they are likely to demand increased medication or changes in medication, not realizing that persistent symptoms are rarely responsive to medication. Accordingly, this intervention often requires the use of psychosocial and psychoeducational methods. Symptom management training involves learning such skills as self-monitoring, medication compliance, and relapse prevention. It can be taught in individual or group treatment settings. It is a clinician-initiated intervention that involves mutual collaboration to assess, teach–learn, and practice the requisite skills. This intervention proceeds in the following fashion.

First, the clinician assesses and evaluates the type and nature of symptoms experienced by the patient. Symptoms are of three types: (a) persistent symptoms (i.e., chronic, low-grade symptoms not ameliorated by medication), (b) warning symptoms (i.e., symptoms gradually increasing in intensity that precede an acute episode), and (c) acute symptoms (i.e., the full-blown incapacitating symptoms that often signal acute decompensation). The nature of symptoms includes both their intensity and duration.

Second, the clinician works with the patient to increase his or her awareness and understanding of the types and nature of symptoms and the skills necessary to effectively manage symptoms. The patient is taught the self-monitoring skill of identifying the type of symptom and intensity (i.e., rates and logs on a 5-point scale: 1 = *mild*, 5 = *very severe*), and duration (logs the amount of time in minutes and number of times the symptom types occur each day for 1 week).

Third, an intervention is planned and tailored to the particular type and expression of symptoms experienced by the individual. Accordingly, acute symptoms are usually treated with medication or medication combined with an individual or group psychosocial or psychoeducational treatment. Psychoeductional methods vary from learning activities and formats that include videotapes, role playing, and homework assignments. Because warning symptoms can result from insufficient medication levels, it is useful to raise medication levels or consider adding an additional medication. Because warning symptoms can result from stopping or decreasing medication, it is essential to inquire about medication noncompliance, which may necessitate checking with a caretaker or significant other. On the other hand, persistent symptoms seldom suggest insufficient medication levels or noncompliance. Thus, they do not require changing dosage or drug regimen, but rather psychoeducational methods such as distraction techniques. For example, the individuals with low-level but chronic dysphoria might achieve considerable relief by distracting themselves from the low energy and blue mood by listening to uplifting or energetic music or watching a funny video movie.

Fourth, the patient practices the interventions (i.e., rating and logging symptoms) and distraction techniques for a given time frame and reports the results at the next meeting with the clinician.

Resource

Liberman, R. (1988). *Social and independent living skills: Symptom management module: Trainers manual.* Los Angeles: Rehabilitation Research.

Thought Stopping

Thought stopping is a self-control intervention to block and/or eliminate ruminative or intrusive thought patterns that are unproductive or anxiety-producing. It may also have the effect of increasing the patient's sense of control and reducing distress. This intervention is usually introduced and demonstrated by the clinician. It is then practiced and applied by the individual. As a result of applying this intervention the individual increases his sense of control. The intervention proceeds in the following fashion.

First, the clinician instructs the client on the similarities between normal and obsessive/intrusive thoughts. An agreement is reached to try to reduce the duration of the intrusive thoughts, thus making them more "normal" and increasing the client's sense of control.

Second, the clinician and client draw up a list of three obsessional thoughts and several specific triggering scenes. Then a list of up to three alternative thoughts (i.e., interesting or relaxing thoughts) is made. For example, a scene from a movie, lying on a sandy beach, or taking a walk through the woods. Each obsessional thought is rated for the discomfort it produces on a scale of 1 to 10 (1 = *lowest*, 10 = *highest*).

Third, the clinician demonstrates how to block obsessional thoughts and substitute an alternative thought. The clinician directs the individual to close his eyes and become relaxed with the instruction to raise a hand when the obsessional thought is first experienced. For example: "Sit back and relax and let your eyes close. I'll mention a specific triggering scene to you, and then describe you experiencing an obsessional thought. As soon as you begin to think the thought, raise your hand, even if I'm only describing the scene." The clinician then describes a typical triggering scene, and as soon as the individual raises a hand, the clinician says "Stop!" loudly. The clinician asks the client whether the obsessional thought was blocked and whether the individual was able to imagine the alternative scene in some detail. The discomfort arising from that obsessional thought is then rated on the 1–10 scale.

Fourth, the clinician then leads the client in practicing thought-stopping with different triggering scenes and alternative thoughts, and the discomfort ratings are recorded. Practice continues until the individual can sufficiently block and replace the obsessional thought.

Fifth, the procedure is modified so that following the clinician's description of the triggering scene and obsessive thought, the client says "Stop" and describes the alternative scene. Practice continues until the individual can sufficiently block and replace the obsessional thought.

Sixth, the clinician gives an intrasession assignment (homework) to the client for 15 minutes of practice a day at times when the client is not distressed by intrusive thoughts. A log is kept with ratings of 1 to 10 made of the distress and vividness evoked by the intrusive thought.

Finally, after a week of practice the clinician prescribes the intervention to be used to dismiss mild to moderately distressing thoughts as they occur. The client is instructed that as his sense of control increases, the thoughts, when they occur, will become less distressing (on the 1–10 scale) until the individual experiences little or no concern about them.

Resource

Hawton, K., Salkovskis, P. , Kirk, J., & Clark, D. (Eds.). (1989). *Cognitive behavior therapy for psychiatric problems*. Oxford, England: Oxford University Press.

☐ Summary

Character has been rediscovered as a basic component of personality and as a key factor in the effective treatment of the personality disorders. To the extent that an individual's temperament dimensions or styles are dysregulated, the individual will express distress or be distressing to others. Higher functioning individuals were socialized and learned self-management and relational skills to regulate such style dimensions as impulsivity, labile affects, and aggressivity during the course of normal child and adolescent development. A hallmark of the early development of personality disordered individuals is deficits in some or many of these coping skills. Both structured psychosocial interventions and medication can be useful in regulating or modulating these style dimensions. This chapter has detailed 15 structured treatment intervention strategies that are useful in modulating affective, behavioral and relational, and cognitive styles.

PART

II

SPECIFIC TREATMENT STRATEGIES

The second part of this book focuses on specific treatment strategies for six common personality disorders that are considered reasonably amenable to treatment. There are two parts to this introductory section: An overview of Chapters 4–9 and a set of general guidelines for working with more severe or impaired individuals. This is the common outline for these chapters:

I. DSM-IV Description and Criteria
II. Effective Treatment Strategies
    1. Engagement Strategies
       Initial Session Behavior
       Facilitating Collaboratioin
       Transference/Countertransference
    2. Pattern Analysis Strategies
       Optimal Criteria
       Schema/Character
       Style/Temperament
    3. Pattern Change Strategies
       Schema/Character Change
       Style/Temperament Change
       Medication
       Group/Family/Couple
       Combined/Integrative
    4. Pattern Maintenance/Termination Strategies
       Termination Issues
       Relapse Prevention
III. Summary
IV. Case Example
V. References
VI. Tables

☐ An Overview of Chapters 4–9

The first section on DSM-IV Description and Criteria presents the DSM-IV description and criteria for the particular disorder.

The second section describes the treatment process and effective strategies for treating each of the personality disorders considered amenable to treatment. Engagement, pattern identification, pattern change, and pattern maintenance refer to the stages of the treatment process from which specific effective strategies have been derived to guide treatment.

The subsection on Engagement describes relationship factors that are likely to be encountered with individuals manifesting this disorder. Specific behaviors that are likely to be manifest in the initial session are described. Specific challenges that the clinician must face in facilitating a working alliance or therapeutic collaboration are noted, as well as the most common transferences and countertransferences.

The subsection on Pattern Analysis Strategies describes optimal criteria, schemas, and style/skills dimensions for each disorder. The optimal single criterion for each disorder is given. Obviously, the diagnosis of personality disorders would be easier if clinicians had only one criterion to remember for each personality disorder. *Schemas* refer to the patient's core beliefs about self and world. Schemas reflect the characterological dimension of the disorder. *Style* refers to the temperament or stylistic dimension of the personality disorder, whereas *skills* refers to the type and level of self-regulation skills and social skills and skill deficits most characteristic of a particular personality disorder.

The subsection on Pattern Change Strategies describes several therapeutic interventions and methods for changing schemas or modifying characterological dimensions of the particular disorder. It also provides a number of treatment methods for modifying the stylistic or temperament dimensions that are under- or overmodulated for a given disorder. Typically, treatment is initially directed at modulating or regulating dysregulated dimensions of temperament that increase the patient's readiness and availability to engage in therapeutic change directed at character dimension of the disorder. Finally, other modalities that are useful and necessary for treatment effectiveness are briefly described.

The subsection on Pattern Maintenance and Termination Strategies offers specific suggestions and directions on terminating the treatment process and preventing relapse. Although premature termination is common among personality disordered individuals, it is less common when treatment is tailored. Nevertheless, planned termination of treatment is particularly difficult with certain personality disorders. More so than with the

Axis I or symptom disorders, a tailored relapse prevention plan is an absolutely essential treatment strategy with Axis II or personality disorders.

The Case Example section translates the many ideas and strategies
previously described into clinical practice. An in-depth case example illustrates how engagement strategies, pattern analysis strategies, pattern change
strategies, and pattern maintenance and termination strategies were used
in an actual case. It goes without saying that, to ensure confidentiality,
details of the case have been modified.

☐ Guidelines for Modifying Treatment Strategy Based on the Patient's Severity of Symptoms or Impairment of Functioning

Throughout Chapters 4–9 several specific treatment strategies will be suggested and described. Many of these strategies are illustrated with specific
case material. The challenge of anyone teaching or writing about psychiatric treatment is to articulate general and specific principles and methods
so that these principles and methods can be reasonably applicable to a
variety of patients. As the cases of Keri and Cindy (described in the Introduction) demonstrate, individuals with personality disorders can present
with widely different levels of symptom severity and functional impairment. The clinician's task is to choose, combine, and tailor therapeutic
interventions to optimize treatment process and outcome. Unfortunately,
texts cannot effectively teach this skill of combining and tailoring treatment strategies. At best, only general guidelines for working with the more
symptomatic and/or impaired personality disordered individuals can be
offered. Here are four such guidelines that might be useful.

First, specify the type and degree of symptoms severity and impairment of functioning. Severity and impairment can be focal or global. Furthermore, both severity and impairment change: There is either a movement toward improvement—which may or may not be related to treatment—or, what is not uncommon among personality disordered patients,
there may be a pattern of waxing and waning of one or both. Therefore, it
is useful to assess the type and degree of both. A strong case can be made
for adopting a standardized or self-developed assessment or rating system
and using it regularly with personality disordered patients. As health care
continues to demand greater accountability in the form of treatment outcome data, this kind of routine rating of a patient's symptomatic presentation and functional level will be commonplace.

Symptoms should be assessed or rated in terms of subtype and degree. Symptom subtypes include standard categories such as those found in standardized instruments—for example, the SCL–90R (Derogatis, 1977), and Compass–OP (Sperry, Brill, Howard, & Grisson, 1996)—which include adjustment, anxiety, depression, bipolar, obsessive-compulsive, phobia, and psychotic. Symptoms can also be addressed in terms of intensity and duration, as being either acute, warning, or persistent symptoms (Sperry, 1995).

Level of functioning or impairment can also be specified by subtype, such as those used in the Social Security Disability Guidelines or the Compass–OP. These include family, health, intimate relationships, self-management, social relationships, and occupational (work, school, home). Kennedy (1992) developed a rating system that elaborates the GAF Scale of Axis V of the DSM-IV. His categories are social skills, dangerousness, occupational, and substance abuse, as well as an overall rating of psychological impairment.

Second, on the basis of this assessment of severity and impairment, establish a problem list. The problem list should be focused, specific, and workable. Symptoms and functional areas are viewed as treatment targets. The more the patient is symptomatic or experiencing impairment, the more structured treatment should become. As such, treatment functions as a "holding environment" that is itself therapeutic.

Third, on the basis of this treatment list, focus treatment accordingly. A basic premise of this book is that focused treatment tends to be more effective with symptomatic or lower functioning personality disordered individuals than generic treatment. A related premise is that as tailored and integrative modalities become increasingly necessary, the level of treatability is lowered. Accordingly, treatment with difficult patients should focus on ameliorating a specific symptom or a specific area of functioning. For symptom management, it may mean introducing medication, increasing dosage, or changing to or adding another medication. Or it may mean using a specific behavioral intervention as the main intervention or as an adjunctive to medication.

To decrease functional impairment, it almost certainly means combining treatment. Usually, this means changing to a more behavioral focus; that is, behavioral rehearsal, social skills training, etc. It may also mean adding additional modalities based on the cognitive and emotional styles and treatment expectations of the patient. Treatment delivered in combination can have an additive, and sometimes synergystic, effect. Traditional modalities like group, family, or couple sessions may be useful, but so may referral to a support group such as Alcoholics Anonymous, Recovery, Inc., groups, or groups sponsored by the National Depressive and Manic Depressive Association. It may just as likely mean "environmental engineering" (i.e., encouraging a patient to leave an abusive relationship or move out of a living situation that fosters substance abuse or dependence).

Fourth, continue monitoring severity and impairment during the course of treatment. Ongoing data collection can prove extremely useful when working with severely disordered individuals. Being able to visually represent the trends of symptoms and functioning over the course of several sessions can be quite revealing for both patient and clinician. Patterns might emerge that otherwise could be missed. For example, increased symptomatology may be found to be related to previously unrecognized circumstances, thoughts, or relationships. Or one particular area of functional impairment, such as work, may continue to lag behind other areas yet never have been seriously addressed in sessions. Charting out the changes in both symptom subtypes and degree, as well as functional subtypes and degrees, may be a useful prognostic guide. If there is little or no change after several sessions, it may indicate that the goals of treatment, treatment strategy, and/or the patient's motivation for change be reviewed. These are some general clinical guidelines to keep in mind while reading and applying the specific guidelines in the following chapters.

CHAPTER 4

Avoidant Personality Disorder

Avoidant personalities are aloof, ill at ease, awkward, and hypersensitive individuals with low self-esteem. Although they are desperate for interpersonal involvement, they avoid personal contact with others because of their heightened fear of social disapproval and rejection. Needless to say, the treatment of avoidant personalities involves a number of unique therapeutic challenges. Nevertheless, these individuals can be effectively treated. As in the rest of this book, the chapter describes specific engagement, pattern analysis, pattern change, and pattern maintenance and termination strategies for effectively managing and treating this disorder. In addition to individual psychotherapeutic strategies and tactics, group, marital and family, medication, and integrative and combined treatment strategies are detailed. An extensive case example illustrates the treatment process. Before turning to treatment strategies, the DSM-IV description and criteria are briefly presented.

☐ DSM-IV Description and Criteria

DSM-IV offers the following description and criteria for the avoidant personality disorder:

TABLE 4.1.   DSM-IV Description and Criteria for Avoidant Personality
Disorder

301.82 Avoidant Personality Disorder

"A pervasive pattern of social inhibition, feelings of inadequacy, and hyper-sensitivity to negative evaluation, beginning by early adulthood and present in a variety of contexts, as indicated by at least four of the following:

(1) avoids occupational activities that involve significant interpersonal contact because of fears of criticism, disapproval, or rejection

(2) is unwilling to get involved with people unless certain of being liked

(3) shows restraint within intimate relationships because of the fear of being shamed or ridiculed

(4) is preoccupied with being criticized or reject in social situations

(5) is inhibited in new interpersonal situations because of feelings of inadequacy

(6) views self as socially inept, personally unappealing, or inferior to others

(7) is unusually reluctant to take personal risks or to engage in any new activities because they may prove embarrassing"

Reprinted with permission from the *Diagnostic and Statistical Manual of Mental Disorders,* Fourth Edition. Copyright 1994, American Psychiatric Association.

☐   Engagement Strategies

Early Session Behavior

In the initial session, these patients are likely to be somewhat guarded and disengaged. Initially, their communication style tends to be monotonic and monosyllabic, and perhaps even circumstantial. Some will appear suspicious or quite anxious, but all are hypersensitive to rejection and criticism. Accordingly, they will observe the clinician closely for any indication of acceptance or rejection. Such reluctance and guardedness should be approached with empathy and reassurance. The clinician would do well to avoid confrontation, which these patients will interpret as criticism. Rather, the clinician's judicious use of empathic responding encourages sharing of past pain and anticipatory fears. When these patients feel that clinicians understand their hypersensitivity and will protect them, they become considerably more willing to trust and cooperate with treatment. After feeling safe and accepted, the atmosphere of the interview changes dramatically. When sufficent rapport has been established, they are more comfortable in describing their fears of being embarrassed and criticized, as well as their sensitivity to being misunderstood. They may experience these fears of being embarrassed as silly and express it. However, to the extent to which clinicians retreat from this empathic and accepting stance, these individuals are likely to feel ridiculed and withdraw again (Othmer & Othmer, 1994).

Facilitating Collaboration

Although the process of achieving collaboration with the avoidant patient tends to be both difficult and protracted, it is well worth the effort. Basic to the difficulty in achieving collaboration is the avoidant patient's tendency to "test" the clinician and the treatment process and the tendency toward premature termination. Because of their underlying sensitivity to criticism and their mistrust of people, these patients have become masters of testing their psychological environment to ascertain which individuals will be positive or at least neutral toward them, and which individuals are likely to criticize, tease, or emotionally challenge them. Usually, there may be a very small number of persons—usually a family member and a friend or colleague—in whom they feel somewhat comfortable to be with and trust to some degree. However, they tend to be rather uncomfortable and distrusting of most individuals, including new clinicians. Subsequently, they will test new clinicians in early sessions by changing appointment dates and times, canceling at the last minute, coming late for sessions, or failing to do homework. The testing continues until they become convinced that the clinician's initial noncritical and nonjudgmental behavior is more than social veneer that falls away when challenged. Beneath this testing is the belief that people really are basically uncaring and critical. To the extent to which the clinician is able to remain supportive, caring, and uncritical in the initial sessions in the face of this testing, the avoidant becomes more amenable to establishing a tentative bond and trust with the clinician. Only then does collaboration become possible. On the other hand, to the extent that the clinician "fails" these tests, the clinician should not be surprised about premature termination. If there is even the slightest hint that a patient is rejection-sensitive or mistrustful, the clinician would do well to anticipate that the patient will engage in testing behaviors and respond accordingly, particularly with unconditional regard.

Transference and Countertransference

The most common transference of the avoidant patient is testing the clinician's capacity to be nonjudgmental and caring. As noted in the section above, this transference is very common in initial sessions. Accepting and sometimes interpreting—particularly through a predictive intepretation—the patient's testing behavior can be useful. Once the clinician passes the various tests of being caring and nonjudgmental, the avoidant patient tends to become increasingly trusting of the clinician. Needless to say, the clinician's stance of unconditional regard is so attractive to these patients that the clincian may be perceived by them as their confidant and most trusted friend. Accordingly, the clinician's task is to resist the exclusivity of this role, and work toward broadening the patient's social support system.

Later in the treatment process, over dependence on the clinician is commonly noted. The avoidant patient may also endeavor to have the clinician assume responsibility for many or all of their personal decisions. The clinician's challenge is to gently but firmly set limits on the patient's dependency.

Common countertransferences are the clinician' s feelings of frustration at the patient's testing behavior. There is also a brittle quality to these patients that may arouse the clinician's rescue fantasies. In the era of managed care, it is not uncommon for these countertransferences to be provoked in situations when clinical protocols emphasize patient engagement and/or require setting treatment goals in the very first session. In these situations, the patient's brittleness and proclivity to premature termination clearly must come before the protocol. As the avoidant patient becomes more involved in the collaborative treatment process, the clinician may fall prey to unrealistic expectations of the patient with regard to increased social involvement. The clinician may erroneously assume that because the patient has been able to establish such a trusting relationship with the clinician, that it can be replicated with others. Monitoring these feeling and urges rather than acting on them is necessary for effective treatment.

☐ Pattern Analysis Strategies

Pattern analysis with avoidant personality disordered individuals involves an accurate diagnostic and clinical evaluation of schemas, styles, and triggering stressors as well as level of functioning and readiness for therapeutic change. Knowledge of the optimal DSM-IV criterion along with the maladaptive pattern of the avoidant personality disordered individual is not only useful in specifying diagnosis but also in planning treatment that is tailored to the histrionic patient's unique style, needs, and circumstances. The optimal criterion specified for the avoidant personality disorder is avoidance of occupational activities that involve significant interpersonal contact because of fear of criticism, disapproval, or rejection (Allnutt & Links, 1996). Both planned treatment goals and interventions should reflect this theme of fear of rejection and anticipatory avoidance.

Pattern refers to the predictable and consistent style and manner in which avoidant individuals think, feel, act, cope, and defend themselves. Pattern analysis involves both the triggers and response—the "what"—as well as an explanatory statement—the "why"—about the pattern of a given avoidant patient. Obviously, such a clinical formulation specifies the particular schemas and temperamental styles unique to a given individual rather than the more general clinical formulation that will be noted here.

Triggers

Generally speaking, the "triggers" or "triggering" situations for avoidant patients are stressors related to close relationships and public appearance (Othmer & Othmer, 1994). This means that when avoidant-disordered individuals are engaging in behaviors, discussing, or even thinking about the demands of relationships or being in public and they become distressed, their disordered or maladaptive pattern is likely to be triggered and their characteristic symptomatic affects, behaviors, and cognitions will be experienced or exhibited. Rather than face the demands of others and risking humiliation and rejection, avoidant individuals prefer to place themselves in safe, rejection-free environments. Usually, this means being alone or in a low-demand social environment.

Schemas

The underlying schemas in the avoidant personality involve a self-view of social inadequacy and unlikability, and a view of the world as unfair, critical, and demeaning alongside a demand that others like and accept the avoidant individual (Beck, Freeman, & Associates, 1990; Sperry & Mosak, 1996). Not surprisingly, the avoidant's dysfunctional strategy is to avoid valuative situations as well as unpleasant feelings or thoughts. Common maladaptive schemas observed in avoidant personality disordered individuals include the defectiveness/shame schema and the undesirability/ alienation schema. The defectiveness/shame schema refers to the core set of beliefs that one is inwardly defective and flawed, and thus basically unlovable and unacceptable. The undesirability/alienation schema refers to the core set of beliefs that one is outwardly different from others or is undesirable to others (Bricker, Young, & Flanagan, 1993).

Style/Temperament

There are three style temperament and skill dimensions: affective, behavioral–interpersonal, and cognitive. Avoidant personality disordered patients have affective styles characterized as shy, tense, apprehensive, and highly vulnerable to rejection and humiliation. Their behavioral and interpersonal style is characterized by social withdrawal, shyness, and under-assertive communication. Their cognitive style is one of hypervigilance and self-doubt as they scan their emotional environment searching for clues of either unconditional acceptance or potential rejection.

☐ Pattern Change Strategies

Generally speaking, the overall goals of treatment with avoidant personality disordered individuals are to increase their capacity to tolerate feedback from others and become more selectively trusting of others. That means that instead of automatically assuming that others intend to criticize, reject, or humiliate them, or reflexively "testing" the trustworthiness of others, avoidant individuals will be able to take some measured risks in relating to others. This might mean assertively communicating their needs and wants, or it might mean taking the risk of requesting some feedback from others who previously have been supportive of them.

Avoidant patients already know how to relate to a small and select number of individuals, often relatives. If the clinician simply becomes one of them, the patient's basic pattern of avoidance may remain unchanged. It is only when these patients learn to recognize the impact of their pattern on others and take risks in new relationships that they can change.

Although individual therapy can help avoidant patients recognize and analyze their pattern of avoidance and withdrawal, couples therapy and group therapy permit both clinician and patient to observe the impact of this pattern on others, and for the patient to risk new behaviors. If the patient is married or in a long-term relationship, triangular patterns are often present. For instance, the avoidant patient may be married to a spouse who travels extensively and makes few if any emotional demands on their avoidant partner, providing the avoidant partner the opportunity for a secret extramarital affair. This triangular pattern provides some degree of intimacy as well as protection from public humiliation, while also insuring interpersonal distance.

Schema Change

The schemas of avoidant patients include themes of defectiveness, inadequacy, and unlikability. These schemas are supported by injunctive beliefs such as "don't show your feelings," "don't get close to others," "don't get intimate," and "don't be disloyal to your family" (Beck, Freeman, & Associates, 1990). Schema change from a cognitive therapy perspective has the clinician and patient working collaboratively to understand the developmental roots of the maladaptive schemas. Then these schemas are tested through predictive experiments, guided observation, and reenactment of early schema-related incidents. Finally, patients are directed to begin to notice and remember counter-schema data about themselves and their social experiences.

Style-Skill Change

Because avoidant patients avoid thinking about matters that cause unpleasant emotions they may report that their minds "go blank" or, they may shift topics when they experience more than mild emotions during sessions. Increasing emotional tolerance is an early treatment goal. This can be accomplished by affect regulation training in which patients are helped to become aware of and "stay with" their distressing thoughts and fantasies. Repeated experiences of "staying with" strange emotions engender emotional tolerance and desensitize their hypersensitivity while at the same time modifying maladaptive beliefs about experiencing uncomfortable emotions.

Avoidant patients tend to exhibit a cognitive style of hypervigilance that results in cognitive avoidance, just as they avoid unpleasant thoughts. These unpleasant thoughts include both those from early childhood and current concerns, such as job and household responsibilities, and especially treatment-related issues like intersession assignment and activities. They may even report that they are unaware of any thoughts during anxiety producing situations, particularly interpersonal situations. Instead they describe their internal experiences in terms of fleeting, negatively tinged sensations or images. In such instances, the clinician should encourage the patients to provide verbatim accounts of what was said and done. Prompting this endeavor will assist the patient in identifying such cognition. In time, the patient will become more able and willing to "stay with" experiences rather than "shutting down." Sensitivity reduction training can also be useful in desensitizing hypervigilance.

Avoidant patients have social skill deficits because of their relational style and their impoverished social experience. These can range from a few circumscribed social deficits to multiple deficits encompassing most social interactions. Alden (1992) listed several types of deficits: (a) behavioral avoidance, wherein patients turn down invitations, cancel appointments, or avoid answering the phone; (b) inhibition, whereby these patients avoid eye contact, initiate few conversations, and talk less than others; (c) surface agreement and compliance, wherein they are likely to voice agreement and comply with the requests of others even when they don't endorse the plan or intend to follow through; (d) assumption of a moderate position, meaning they avoid taking a stand or expressing their own opinion in issues; (e) and absence of self-disclosure, wherein, because of their belief that they are defective, they are extremely anxious about revealing personal information and do not reciprocate the self-disclosures of others.

Assertive communication training can be used to teach patients to think and speak more assertively and with a "non-avoidant voice." Interpersonal skills training can be useful in reversing some of these skill deficits, as well as modifying their shy, inhibited style. In the psychotherapeutic setting, these patients may need to be encouraged to act "as if" they are confident, assertive, and likable.

Medication Strategies

Many avoidant personality disordered patients fear medication and its side effects just as they do any other new experience. Nevertheless, medication can be useful in modulating some style dimensions, particularly rejection sensitivity. Phenelzine and other MAO inhibitors have been used effectually with reducing hypersensitivity and increasing emotional tolerance (Deltito & Stam, 1989). The new generation of MAO inhibitors, known as reversible inhibitors of MAO (RIMA), particularly brofaromia and moclobemide, have been shown to be quite effective in patients with presentations of social phobia that resemble avoidant personality disorder (Liebowitz, Schneier, Hollander, et al., 1991).

Furthermore, these medications are also useful in ameliorating anxious symptoms that often are comorbid with avoidant personality disorder. Finally, serotonin blockers and MAOI agents have been noted to be useful in treating the features of the avoidant personalty disorder that resemble social phobia (Siever & Davis, 1991).

Group Treatment Strategies

Avoidant personality disordered patients typically fear group therapy in the same way they fear other novel and socially demanding situations. As a result of taking measured risk of self-disclosure and receiving feedback from other group members, avoidant individuals can greatly modify their social sensitivity. For this reason, group therapy is particularly effective for avoidant patients who can be persuaded to undergo this mode of treatment. Empathetic group therapy can assist these individuals in overcoming social anxieties and developing interpersonal trust and rapport.

Because avoidant individuals tend to avoid activities that involve significant interpersonal contact for fear of being exposed or ridiculed, it should not be surprising that it takes longer for them to adapt to a group setting and actively participate in treatment. Accordingly, combining cognitive therapy and social skills training in a group-therapy context can be quite effective in identifying underlying fears, increasing awareness of the anxiety related to fears, and shifting attentional focus from fear-related thinking to behavioral action. The group therapist's role in pacing the avoidant patient's disclosure and engagement within the group can be very important. Structured activities can help the avoidant individuals to organize how they think and act so they are more efficient both inside and outside the therapy context. For example, interpersonal skills training that focuses on the process of friendship formation is particularly well-suited for group treatment contexts (Sperry, 1995).

Marital and Family Therapy Strategies

Although there is value in recognizing how their current dysfunctional patterns were developed, the real measure of treatment success with avoidant individuals is improvement in interpersonal functioning. Because avoidant patients may provide clinicians with vague descriptions of their interpersonal experiences, it may be necessary to query relatives and significant others to fill in the important gaps of information. Family treatment may be indicated to establish a family structure that allows more room for interpersonal exploration outside the tightly closed family circle. Furthermore, couples therapy is indicated for avoidant individuals in marriages or long-term relationships where intimacy problems are prominent, that is, where interpersonal distance characterizes the avoidant partner's relational style and is the source of conflict (Sperry, 1995).

Combined and Integrative Treatment Strategies

Clinical experience suggests that avoidant individuals are often unable to focus on the patient–clinician relationship to the degree necessary to use traditional psychodynamic approaches. Likewise, these patients may have difficulty fully using cognitive-behavioral interventions in the interpersonal context of therapy. Accordingly, an integrative treatment strategy may be more appropriate. Alden (1992) described an integration of the cognitive and the psychodynamic-interpersonal approaches that has been developed specifically for the treatment of avoidant personality dynamics. This approach focuses on modifying the cognitive-interpersonal patterns of the avoidant personality, which is characterized by dysfunctional beliefs of being different or defective and that these defects and feelings are obvious to others who will respond with disgust, disapproval, or dismissal.

Alden (1992) described four steps in the integrative approach. The first step is recognition of treatment process issues. The clinician must quickly recognize that these patients tend to withhold or understate information that is clinically relevant. It should be anticipated that these patients will respond to direct questions with "I don't know" or "I'm not sure" answers. In the early phase of treatment, such noncommital and evasive responses characterizes their thought processes as well as prevents them from encoding details about social encounters. Rather then interpreting "resistance" or focusing on global and vague interpersonal beliefs and behavior as treatment targets, the clinician can simply recognize that this communication style reflects their inability to process positive information, maintain attentiveness, and change their firmly established negative beliefs and schemas.

Treatment then focuses on increasing awareness of cognitive-interpersonal patterns. There are four components to an interpersonal pattern: beliefs and expectancy of the other person; the behavior that arises from these beliefs; the other person's reaction; and the conclusion drawn from the experience. The patient's task is to engage in a process of self-observation and analysis of their relational patterns, whereas the clinician's task is to draw attention to the beliefs that underlie the patient's self-protective behaviors.

Next, as they come to recognize and to understand their cognitive-interpersonal patterns and styles, the clinician can increase their motivation to try new behavior by helping them recognize that old and new views of self are in conflict, and that such conflict can be reconciled. Assisting patients integrate their current beliefs with their earlier interpersonal experiences helps them understand that their social fears and expectations resulted from both their experience of being parented and their temperament. As they continue to recognize and understand their cognitive-interpersonal patterns, these individuals begin to try different strategies, either on their own or with the clinician's prompting. Step 4 involves behavioral experimentation and cognitive evaluation. Friendship formation and assertive communication are the two basic interpersonal skills that avoidant patients must increase. Role playing and directed assignments are particularly useful in developing assertive communication skills (Sperry, 1995).

A basic premise of this book is that although a single treatment modality like psychotherapy may well be effective for the highest functioning personality disordered individual, that modality is less effective for moderate functioning and largely ineffective for more severely dysfunctional individuals. For the most part, lower functioning patients tend to be more responsive to combined treatment modalities. Even though avoidant patients initially are reluctant to engage in group therapy, moderate and lower functioning avoidant patients tend to make considerable progress when involved in both individual and group therapy concurrently. When this is not possible, time-limited skill-oriented group training sessions or a support group may be sufficient. Because their pattern of avoidance and social inhibition makes entry into and continuation with therapeutic groups distressing, individual sessions can be focused on transitioning the patient into the group. Finally, medication may be necessary in the early stages of treatment, and can be particularly useful in reducing distress and self-protective behavior during the transition into concurrent group treatment.

☐ Pattern Maintenance and Termination Strategies

Termination Issues

Termination can be particularly problematic for avoidant patients. Although these patients were prone to premature termination in the initial phase of treatment, once they become engaged in the treatment process they often find it difficult to face planned termination. For this reason, it is essential that the treatment plan include provision for weaning therapy in the final phase. Avoidant patients typically need prompting and encouragement to test out their fears about reducing the frequency of sessions. Occasionally, some avoidant patients are ready and willing to terminate but may fear hurting the clinician's feelings by suggesting or readily agreeing that they are ready for termination.

Spacing out sessions allows patients to deal with and discuss their fear, particularly regarding rejection. It also allows them the opportunity to engage in new social and interpersonal experiences between sessions and deal with the risks attendant to such experiences. Perhaps if they were on medication and involved in weekly individual or group therapy; they might now have scheduled medication monitoring appointments at 3- to 6-month intervals already. If they were not receiving, or have already been weaned from, medication they might have booster sessions scheduled at 3-, 6-, or 12-months intervals.

Finally, it is helpful for clinicians and avoidant patients to collaboratively develop a plan of self-therapy and self-management following termination. It is recommended that these patients set aside an hour a week to engage in activities that continue the progress made in formal treatment. They could look for any situations they might have avoided that week and analyze obstacles and thoughts that interfered. Or they might look ahead at the coming week and predict which situations could be troublesome, and plan ways to cope with possible avoidance behaviors. The goal of such effort is, of course, to maintain treatment gains and maintain the newly acquired pattern.

Relapse Prevention Strategies

Another essential aspect of the treatment plan and process is relapse prevention. Because avoidant patients can easily revert to their previous avoidant pattern, it is necessary to predict and plan for relapse. The final phase of treatment should largely focus on relapse prevention. An important goal of relapse prevention is predicting likely difficulties in the time period immediately following termination. The patient needs to be able to analyze specific external situations such as new individuals, unfamiliar places, as well as internal states such as specific avoidant beliefs and fears, and other vulnerabilities that increase the likelihood of them responding with avoidant behavior in the face of predictable triggers. Once predicted, patients can develop a contingency plan to deal with these stressors. Clinicians may find it useful to have avoidant patients think and talk through the following questions: What can I do if I find myself resorting to avoidant patterns? What should I do if I start believing my old avoidant beliefs more than my new beliefs? What should I do if I relapse?

A belief that is particularly troubling for avoidant patients is, "If others really knew me, they would reject me." This belief is typically activated when avoidant patients begin developing new relationships or when they begin to self-disclose at a deeper level with individuals they already know. In such instances, it can be helpful for patients to view these fears of revealing themselves with a trusted person to trace what actually happened when they were eventually able to self-disclose. Finally, a relapse prevention plan will specify specific outcome goals and activities for the post-termination period: Usually, these goals involve establishing new friendships, deepening existing relationships, acting more assertively, tackling previously avoided social tasks, and trying new experiences such as volunteering or attending a workshop alone.

☐ Case Example

Cindy K. is a moderately obese, 41-year-old, never-married, White female administrative assistant who presented with a 3-week onset of sad mood, loss of appetite, insomnia, and increasing social isolation. She had not showed up for work for 4 days prompting the clinical intervention. Cutbacks at her office led to a transfer from the accounting department—a small and close-knit group—where she had been for 11 years, to a similar position working in a much larger, diverse department at another location.

Engagement Process

She had missed the first appointment for the initial evaluation and had come late for the second with the explanation that she could not find the clinic. She indicated she had come only at the insistence of the director of human resources and didn't believe she needed treatment. Self-disclosure was clearly difficult for her. She did, however, view her job transfer as a significant loss and she thought that it might have triggered her depressive symptoms and isolative behavior. There was no indication that she was a danger to herself, and it appeared that outpatient treatment was possible. Because it was anticipated that she would "test" and provoke the clinician into criticizing her for changing or canceling appointments or coming late, and that setting up a follow-up appointment would probably be difficult, the clinician made a predictive interpretation to that effect near the end of the first session. Needless to say, the appointment was made with ease, and Cindy did arrive at her next appointment on time.

Pattern Analysis

No personal or family psychiatric or alcohol and substance abuse history was reported. However, she described intense feelings of humiliation and rejection following the birth of a younger brother, after having been very much spoiled by her parents. She came to believe that the opinions of others were all that counted. Yet she was teased and ridiculed by her peers for her personal appearance, especially her obesity. There were also strong parental injunctions against discussing important matters with "outsiders." It appears that she distances and isolates herself from others, anticipating and fearing their disapproval and criticism. She views others as critical and harsh and is convinced she is viewed by others as inadequate. Therefore, she is slow to warm up and trust others, and "tests" others' trustability by being late for, canceling, or missing agreed on engagements. She had also spent much of her free time reading romance novels, and watching TV rather than going out. Lack of social skills in relating to new or less-known individuals and a limited social network further contributed to an isolated lifestyle and reinforced her beliefs about self, the world, and others. With the exception of social relations, she has functioned above average in all life tasks. She agrees she is severely depressed and wants to cooperate with combined treatment involving medication started and monitored on an outpatient basis along with time-limited psychotherapy. She was not particularly psychologically minded and had significant skill deficits in assertive communication, trust, and relational skills. Nevertheless, she continues to be abstinent for 2 years after completing a smoking cessation program. Her support system includes some contact with an older female friend and a pet collie.

Developmental history data suggested that Cindy had internalized the schemas of defectiveness/shame and social undesirablitity/alienation, which can be associated with the avoidant personality. Her apprehensive affects, hypervigilance, shyness, and deficits in assertiveness and other interpersonal skills were also indicative of the avoidant personality. Her history and mental status exam are consistent with a diagnosis of major depressive disorder—single episode, as well as meeting the criteria for avoidant personality disorder. Figure 4.1 summarizes these style features.

Pattern Change

The treatment plan for Cindy was developed based on her presentation as well as her pattern and prognostic factors. Combined treatment with an antidepressant and psychotherapy focused on ameliorating symptoms, returning to work and establishing a supportive social network, and increasing interpersonal skills were the initial treatment outcome goals established. The treatment and strategic goals were developed to facilitate therapeutic outcomes by maximizing therapeutic leverage while minimizing the influence of previous perpetuants and other forms of resistance to change.

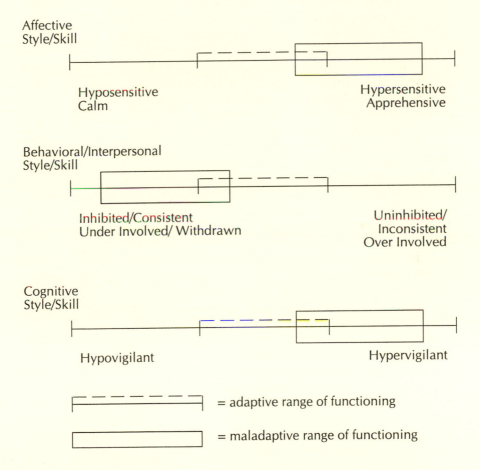

Affective
Style/Skill

Hyposensitive   Hypersensitive
Calm   Apprehensive

Behavioral/Interpersonal
Style/Skill

Inhibited/Consistent   Uninhibited/
Under Involved/ Withdrawn   Inconsistent
                                 Over Involved

Cognitive
Style/Skill

Hypovigilant   Hypervigilant

= adaptive range of functioning

= maladaptive range of functioning

FIGURE 4.1. Style/skill dimensions of avoidant personality disorder.

Treatment consisted of a trial of antidepressant that was sedating and which it was hoped would reverse her insomnia as well as her depression. Twenty-minute weekly outpatient sessions with the psychiatrist focused on symptom reduction and returning to work. This meant that some collaboration with her supervisor about work and peer support was initiated. The supervisor agreed that Cindy needed a familiar, trusting social support, and was able to assign one of Cindy's coworkers to the same office to which she had been moved. An initial treatment agreement was established for six 45-minute sessions combining medication and interpersonal therapy. They also discussed that skill-oriented group therapy was probably the treatment of choice for her to increase trustability and decrease her social isolation. Aware that her pattern of avoidance would make entry into and continuation with the group difficult, the plan was for the individual sessions to serve as a transition into group, after which shorter individual sessions would focus on medication management, probably on a monthly and then bimonthly basis.

Knowing her pattern, the clinician anticipated that she would test the clinician and group therapist's trustability and criticalness. Throughout treatment both clinicians continued to be mindful of the therapeutic leverage—her strengths and previous success with smoking cessation—as well as the perpetuants that would likely hamper treatment.

The initial treatment plan for her involved the combined modalities of medication management and a short course in interpersonal psychotherapy for depression with gradual transition into a time-limited group therapy focused on interpersonal skill development. As her depressive symptoms ameliorated and a maintenance medication schedule was established, the clinician began preparing her for transition into the group. Because of Cindy's fear and ambivalence of the group process, the clinician suggested and she agreed that it might be helpful to meet with the group therapist who leads the interpersonal skills group she was slated to join. During their fifth session, the group therapist was briefly introduced to Cindy and discussion of a three-way treatment agreement. The three agreed that Cindy would continue in individual weekly appointments concurrent with weekly group session. And assuming things were proceeding well enough, sessions with the prescribing clinician would be reduced to monthly medication checks.

A subsequent two-way discussion between group therapist and clinician concluded that there was little likelihood that projective identification and splitting would be issues with her. Instead, difficulty maintaining active group participation and follow-up on "homework" between group sessions were predicted. The clinician agreed to encourage and support the patient's group involvement in his concurrent individual sessions with her. Furthermore, the group therapist and clinician planned on conferring after the third group session regarding the transition from weekly to monthly sessions with the clinician.

Pattern Maintenance and Termination

Treatment proceeded with few surprises. Her depressive symptoms were ameliorated within 5 weeks and she was continued on a maintenance dose for a period of 1 year. Medication monitoring sessions were reduced to monthly visits for the first 4 months and then bimonthly afterward. Progress in group sessions included increased confidence in social situations, especially in her job setting. After 6 months of weekly group sessions she felt ready to terminate and continued with bimonthly sessions with the prescribing clinician. She still maintains some interpersonal reserve but she is able to socialize regularly with two other female coworkers. Her job performance gradually returned to baseline.

☐ Summary

Effective treatment of the avoidant personality disorder requires that these patients become sufficiently committed to a treatment process that is tailored and focused on modifying their maladaptive avoidant pattern. Because these patients tend to have considerable difficulty engaging in and profiting from traditional psychotherapy, an integrative-combined approach, which focuses on characterological, temperament and skill dimensions, is usually essential for effective treatment outcomes. The case example illustrates the common challenges that these patients present, and the kind of clinician flexibility and competence as well as treatment resources required. Table 4.2 summarizes the treatment intervention strategies most likely to be effective with this disorder.

TABLE 4.2. Treatment Strategies with Avoidant Personality Disorder

Phase	Issues	Strategy/Tactics
Engagement	Premature termination; "Testing" behavior: canceling appointments/ difficulty scheduling; Distrust clinician's caring and fear of rejection Difficulty with self-disclosure	Anticipate patient's trust "testing"
Transference	"Testing"; Overdependence	Accept and interpret "testing" behaviors; Set limits on dependency
Countertransference	Frustration and helplessness Unrealistic treatment expectations	Monitor
Pattern Analysis	**Triggers:** Close relationships and public appearance	
Pattern Change	**Treatment Goals:** Better tolerate feedback; Become more selectively trusting	
Schemas	Defectiveness/shame; Social undesirability/ alienation	Schema change strategy; Interpretation strategy
Style/Skills		
a. Affective Style	Hypersensitive and apprehensive	Affect regulation

Table 4.2 continues on page 85.

TABLE 4.2. *Continued*

Phase	Issues	Strategy/Tactics
b. Behavioral/ Interpersonal Style	Avoidance/withdrawal behavior; Shyness and under-assertiveness	Interpersonaly skills training; Assertive communication training
c. Cognitive Style	Hypervigilance	Sensitivity reduction training
Maintenance/ Termination	Homework avoidance Anxiety and ambivalence about termination	Daily log/diary; Space out sessions; Booster sessions

Borderline Personality Disorder

Borderline personalities tend to be emotionally labile and impulsive individuals who exhibit a pattern of intense and chaotic relationships. Their personal lives are characteristically unfocused and unstable and are marked by frequent disappointments and rejections. Not surprisingly, the treatment of borderline personalities involves a number of unique therapeutic challenges. Although many clinicians remain skeptical about the treatability of this disorder, there is increasing hopefulness that borderline individuals can and do respond to effective treatment strategies. As in the rest of this book, the chapter describes specific engagement, pattern analysis, pattern change, and pattern maintenance and termination strategies for effectively managing and treating this disorder. In addition to individual psychotherapeutic strategies and tactics, group, marital and family, medication, and integrative and combined treatment strategies are briefly noted. An extensive case example illustrates the treatment process. Before turning to treatment strategies, the DSM-IV description and criteria are briefly presented.

☐ DSM-IV Description and Criteria

DSM-IV offers the following description and criteria for the borderline personality disorder.

86

TABLE 5.1.   DSM-IV Description and Criteria for Borderline
Personality Disorder

301.83 Borderline Personality Disorder

"A pervasive pattern of instability in interpersonal relationships, self-image and affects, and marked impulsivity beginning by early adulthood and present in a variety of contexts, as indicated by five (or more) of the following:

(1) frantic efforts to avoid real or imagined abandonment. (Note: Do not include suicidal or self-mutilating behavior covered in Criterion 5.)

(2) a pattern of unstable and intense interpersonal relationships character-ized by alternating between extremes of idealization and devaluation

(3) identity disturbance: markedly and persistently unstable self-image or sense of self

(4) impulsivity in at least two areas that are potentially self-damaging (e.g., spending, sex, substance abuse, reckless driving, binge eating). (Note: Do not include suicidal or self-mutilating behavior covered in Criterion 5.)

(5) recurrent suicidal behavior, gestures, or threats, or self-mutilating behavior

(6) affective instability due to a marked reactivity of mood (e.g., intense episodic dysphoria, irritability, or anxiety usually lasting a few hours and only rarely more than a few days)

(7) chronic feelings of emptiness

(8) inappropriate, intense anger or difficulty controlling anger (e.g., frequent displays of temper, constant anger, recurrent physical fights)

(9) transient, stress-related paranoid ideation or severe dissociative symptoms"

☐ **Engagement Strategies**

Early Session Behavior

Interviewing individuals with borderline personality features presents clinicians with a special challenge due to the instability and ambivalence of this personality. Lability or instability is present not only in their moods and cognitions, but also in their rapport with the clinician. Instability involving rapport can be handled by empathically focusing on it. This can be accomplished by focusing the discussion, tracking the discussion, and curbing outbursts and diversions. With this patient, open-ended questioning is preferable to closed-ended and pointed questioning. Furthermore, instability can be handled by focusing on its pathological part that needs to be explored. Because instability affects rapport, the clinician should continually acknowledge its presence and effect. As a result of these strategies, borderline patients become less defensive and more willing to disclose, which leads to increased rapport (Othmer & Othmer, 1994).

In a manner similar to the way in which they relate to others, borderline patients will also direct their angry and rageful affects toward clinicians. Experienced clinicians expect borderline patients to relate in this manner at the outset of treatment. Nevertheless, this manner of relating does heighten tension in the therapeutic relationship. Managing this tension and providing the resources to keep the therapeutic relationship at an active working level is a constant challenge in the treatment of these patients (Sperry, 1995).

Dealing with ambivalence requires confronting their contradictory statements while simultaneously displaying an understanding of their ambivalent feelings. They may enthusiastically describe a new relationship one moment and then devalue it in the next when they recall something unpleasant about that relationship. Generally speaking, therapeutic confrontation can effectively neutralize their splitting and projective identification, just as it moderates overidealization and devaluation. Therapeutic confrontation also helps them realize that their ambivalence is the result of a perceived lack of support and understanding from the other person. Finally, therapeutic confrontation permits them to realize—however painful—the extent to which they have allowed others to profoundly influence their sense of well-being (Waldinger, 1987).

Therapeutic confrontation is probably not indicated when there is evidence of childhood sexual and physical abuse in the borderline patient, at least in the early phases of treatment. There is developing literature on how treatment is modified when such abuse issues are present (Gunderson

& Chu, 1993). In fact, some would contend that interpretation of aggressive themes and transference interpretations must be made carefully, if at all, and that the clinician must validate the role of bad parenting in the patient's past as a motivating force for that aggression (Buie & Adler, 1982–1983).

Family members are often incorporated into the treatment process with the expectation that the borderline's self-harmful behavior can be reduced or compliance with medication or other aspects of treatment will be improved. Clinicians should anticipate the emotional response of family members toward the borderline patient whenever they are involved in the treatment process, particularly family treatment sessions. At times, family members may be intrusive and overcontrolling, while rejecting and hostile at other times. This vacillating pattern can significantly complicate the treatment process making family sessions difficult if not impossible. Unless this pattern is therapeutically confronted, family communications will not improve. Nor, is it likely that compliance will increase or that self-harmful behavior be reduced. More on involving family members in treatment is described in a subsequent section (see Marital and Family Strategies).

Facilitating Collaboration

By definition personality disordered individuals find it difficult to cooperate and collaborate, much less take responsibility for their own behavior. This is particularly true for borderline patients who typically enter treatment for the expressed purpose of feeling better rather than making changes in their lives. They want to have their abandonment feelings disappear, their worries soothed, and their problems of daily living resolved. Their secret desire is that someone all powerful and all nurturing will "make up" for their heretofore chaotic and rejection-ravaged life. In short, they believe that it is someone else's responsibility to make everything better for them. It is certainly not their responsibility because they did not create their problem-strewn lives. In the therapeutic setting that "someone" is the clinician.

Limit setting and treatment contracting are two other powerful strategies for achieving engagement. Usually, these strategies are used with lower functioning borderline patients who are parasuicidal or act out in various other ways. Establishing a written contract to avert suicidal behaviors is one of the most common uses. Contracts can be used to facilitate treatment adherence such as attendance for after-care programs, reducing fighting or compulsive behaviors, or increasing medication compliance.

Clinicians should consider the "no treatment option" whenever evaluating treatment requests involving a borderline disordered patient. In this option, borderline patients with a long history of treatment failure are not automatically offered psychotherapy or even medication management when it is requested or demanded (Frances, Clarkin, & Perry (1984). Because of the high likelihood of repeating their failure pattern again and when no noticeable change in readiness for treatment is assessed, the clinician has two options. The first is the offer to reevaluate the patient at a later time when the patient is more ready for treatment. The second is the offer of an extended treatment evaluation of three to four sessions during which the clinician evaluates the patient's readiness for treatment based on their response to prescribed intersession tasks. Compliance with the tasks demonstrates some measure of willingness for collaboration and self-responsibility, and leads to an extension of the treatment contract for an additional set of sessions. This strategy reinforces the patient's success with treatment sessions, rather than reinforcing the patient's failure as in previous treatment episodes. Examples of intersession tasks include keeping a log of symptoms or target behaviors, or accomplishing specific tasks like attending two 12-step meetings and finding a 12-step sponsor within a given time frame.

Another common engagement strategy is establishment of a holding environment, which can refer to the clinician's containment function or to a treatment philosophy in an inpatient or partial hospitalization program. The holding or containing function refers to the clinician's capacity to receive and "hold" the patients' projections without absorbing them or acting them. Furthermore, the clinician is able to mediate these projections back to patients so that they may integrate these parts of themselves that previously were not tolerable, such as anger and rage. Kernberg (1984) described how a holding environment can serve as the operational philosophy in an inpatient unit or partial hospital program for the treatment of borderline personality disordered patients.

Transference and Countertransference

Given that interpersonal relationships tend to be inordinately troublesome for borderline patients, matters involving transference and countertransference should be of considerable concern to the clinician. Transference in borderline patients runs the gamut from helplessness and merger fantasy to scornfulness. Dependency transferences may be the most common. In the dependency transference, the borderline patient relies on the clinician to make decisions and otherwise take responsibility for their well-being.

As noted earlier, this underlying attitude considerably limits treatment progress.

Common clinician countertransferences include anger, guilt, antagonism, fear, rejection, feelings of manipulation, and rescue fantasies. Clinicians can easily become angry because of the borderline's demandingness, overdependency, or acting-out behavior. Obviously, clinicians need to monitor their thoughts and reactions to these patients who are incredibly sensitized to the paralanguage of others. For instance, the clinician can respond to the borderline patient's hostility by saying, "I'm getting the impression you're trying to make me angry at you instead of letting me help you. Let's see if *we* can understand what's happening." Because of the borderline's rejection sensitivity and tendency to feel blamed, it is therapeutically valuable to emphasize the interpersonal nature of the verbal interaction. In addition, clinicians may have to set limits on the patient's hostility so as to hold their own countertransference in check: "I'm not sure *we're* going to accomplish anything if you continue screaming. It's important that you work on controlling your anger so you can express it in a less provocative way."

☐ Pattern Analysis Strategies

Pattern analysis with borderline-disordered individuals involves an accurate diagnostic and clinical evaluation of schemas, styles, and triggering stressors as well as their level of functioning and readiness for therapeutic change. Knowledge of the optimal DSM-IV diagnostic criterion along with the maladaptive pattern of the borderline personality disordered individual is not only useful in specifying diagnosis but also in planning treatment that is tailored to the patient's unique style, needs, and circumstances. The optimal criterion specified for the borderline personality disorder is frantic efforts to avoid real or imagined abandonment (Allnutt & Links, 1996). Borderline personality disordered individuals often respond to abandonment with angry outbursts as well as splitting and projective identification. Self-destructive impulsive behaviors, such as wrist-slashing, overdosing, promiscuity and substance abuse, are common. Fear of abandonment also amplifies ambivalence about relationships, which further interferes with establishing and maintaining stable, enduring relationships. This means that treatment planning must of necessity target these overmodulations of affective style, behavioral style, and cognitive style for intervention.

Pattern refers to the predictable and consistent style and manner in which a patient thinks, feels, acts, copes, and defends the self. Pattern analysis involves both the triggers and response—the "what"—as well as a clinical formulation or explanatory statement—the "why"—about the pattern of a given borderline patient. Obviously, such a clinical formulation specifies the particular schemas and temperamental styles unique to a given individual rather than the more general clinical formulation that will be noted here.

Generally speaking, the "triggers" or "triggering" situations for borderline patients are stressors related to close personal relationships and personal goals. This means that when borderline disordered individuals are engaging in behaviors, discussing, or even thinking about certain relationships or achieving certain personal goals and become distressed, their disordered or maladaptive pattern is likely to be triggered and their characteristic symptomatic affects, behaviors, and cognitions are likely to be experienced or exhibited. Borderline individuals perceive these triggers in typical ambivalent fashion. For instance, the stress of a close relationship may trigger the thought, "People are great, no they are not," while the stress of a personal goal triggers the thought: "Goals are good, no they are not" (Othmer & Othmer, 1994). Whether the individual's full maladaptive pattern, particularly acting-out behavior, ensues is dependent on various situational factors.

Schemas

Generally speaking, the underlying schemas of borderline disordered individuals involve a self view of uncertainty about self-identity, gender, career, and their very worth. Their world view is equally uncertain as they are ambivalent about others' loyalty to them, the stability of the world, and the likelihood that they can make a commitment to anything or anyone (Sperry & Mosak, 1996). Among the most frequently encountered schemas in borderline patients are unloveability/defectiveness, abandonment/loss, and dependency/incompetence (Layden et al., 1993; Young, 1994). The unloveability/defectiveness schema refers to the core belief that one is internally flawed, and if others recognize this they will withdraw from the relationship. The abandonment/loss schema is central to this personality disorder and refers to the expectation that one will imminently lose any and every close relationship. The dependency/incompetence schema refers to the core belief that one is incapable of handling daily responsibilities competently and independently, and so must rely on us to make decisions and initiate new tasks.

Style/Temperament

There are three style/temperament dimensions that may need to be addressed in formulating treatment with the borderline personality: affective, behavioral–interpersonal, and cognitive. Needless to say, these styles exacerbate and are exacerbated by their schemas. Borderline individuals are prone to overmodulated thinking, such as splitting and projective identification. They are also characteristically impulsive, and their affects, particularly moods, tend to be overmodulated. This impulsive style can further exacerbate their proclivity to self-destructive behavior, including self-mutilation. Relationally, because of their history of impulsivity and overmodulated affects, these individuals tend to exhibit limited interpersonal skills, which further exacerbates their schemas of abandonment, unlovability, and incompetence.

☐ Pattern Change Strategies

Generally speaking, the overall goal of treatment is to achieve some measure of stability and cohesiveness. Accomplishing this goal requires a four-fold strategy: (a) reduce symptoms of the Axis I disorder; (b) remodulate problematic temperament/style features such as impulsivity, distress intolerance, and parasuicidality; (c) increase the patient's levels of life functioning; and (d) modify character/schema features. This section describes six different strategies for pattern change: style modulation, medication, schema modification, group treatment modalities, marital and family therapy modalities, and combined/integrative modalities.

Style Change Strategies

For all practical purposes, style modulation strategies include medication and social skills training. Either alone or in combination with rational psychopharmacotherapy, social skills training is an effective strategy for remodulating disordered style dimensions. The goal of this strategy is to achieve sufficient affective, behavioral, and cognitive stability so that the patient will sufficiently be ready and amenable to work on more traditional therapeutic issues.

Needless to say, many borderline disordered individuals have unmodulated styles because they never adequately learned sufficient self-control skills during their formative years. Thus, it becomes necessary for them to reverse these specific skill deficits in the context of treatment. Either within an individual or group treatment context, these skills are learned and practiced. Six different types of skill training are particularly useful for the kind of unmodulated styles most commonly seen in borderline patients. Emotion awareness training and emotional regulation training target overmodulated affects. Impulse control training targets impulse dyscontrol. Self-management training is particularly useful in stemming self-destructive behaviors such as self-mutilation and the multiple forms of parasuicidality. Interpersonal skill training is targeted for a wide range of interpersonal skill deficits including effective communications and making and keeping friends. Cognitive awareness training targets the propensity for splitting and projective identification. Finally, distress tolerance training targets distressing thoughts that the individual can no longer cope with further stressors without incurring disastrous consequences.

Not surprisingly, the course of treatment with borderline patients—particularly those who are lower functioning—can easily become crisis-oriented because of their chaotic pattern. Not only can level of readiness change from session to session, but continuity of therapeutic focus can seldom be maintained from session to session, particularly in the early stages of treatment. For this reason it is useful to be able to assess the patient's level of readiness and specify related and relevant treatment objectives at each session. One way of assessing the patient's readiness at each session is in terms of treatment or intervention targets. This scheme is more sensitive than the stages of readiness for change described in Chapter 1 and is considerably modified from the hierarchy of treatment targets described by Linehan (1993). She described five sets of progressive treatment targets: parasuicidal; behaviors interfering with the conduct of treatment, such as missing sessions or medication noncompliance; escape behaviors that interfere with making or maintaining changes outside of treatment, such as substance abuse or illegal actions; skills acquisition that are necessary to function more effectively in and outside of treatment; and achievement of the patient's personal goals.

Clearly, patients who are parasuicidal or continually acting out in treatment are not as ready for work on schema change as patients who are sufficiently engaged in treatment and have the requisite skills to collaborate in processing regressive issues like emotional and sexual abuse. Table 5.2 list four sets of treatment targets that can serve as both an assessment tool and treatment menu in the early course of treatment. The suggested treatment strategy for using these treatment targets is to assess the patient's current level of treatment readiness and then focus on that level as long as necessary before preceding to the next level. Thus, if the patient reports or

Text continues on page 98.

TABLE 5.2. Intervention Targets Based on Levels of Treatment Readiness

1. Parasuicidal Behavior

   - suicidal plans
   - suicidal gestures (cutting, overdose, etc)
   - intense/frequent suicidal ideation
   - self mutilation (specify)
   - other self injurious behavior (specify)
   - substance dependence/chronic eating disorder
   - engaging in any activities AMA

2. Treatment Threatening Behavior

   - unwillingness to acknowledge and accept psychiatric illness;
   - history of treatment noncompliance/adherence to medications, appointments, staffings;
   - noncompliance with sessions, medications or assigned homework;
   - boundary problems: excessive phone calls, over dependence or over demanding of clinician;
   - demanding focus of treatment be on highly regressive topics before the patient is "ready";
   - coming late for sessions;
   - not following up on agreed plans, volunteer work, etc.

3. Escape Behaviors

   - substance abuse beyond occasional social drinking;
   - anti-social behavior: stealing, prostitution, drugs, child abuse;
   - binging, purging, fasting;
   - other addictive/impulsive behavior;
   - inattentive, "spaced out", internally preoccupied in treatment programs, volunteer work, etc.;
   - teasing, rough housing, non-therapeutically challenging other patients or staff;
   - isolating self from others in treatment program, family, group home, etc, but sitting alone listening to music with earphones, etc.

Table 5.2 continues on page 96.

TABLE 5.2. *Continued*

4. Skills
    +Symptoms Management Skills: Acute Symptoms = abrupt onset of clinical Sx:

    • auditory hallucinations or other hallucinations;
    • delusions: persecution, grandiose, somatic;
    • mania: flight of ideas, high energy, little sleep;
    • depression: sadness, despair, crying spells, anhedonia, disturbed sleep;
    • intense and/or frequent suicidal/homicidal ideation;
    • intense anxiety/panic/compulsive behavior;
    • strong desire for substance use/abuse.

    +Symptoms Management Skills: Persistent Symptoms = chronic, subclinical symptoms:
    Goal = to distract/divert/control through coping skills

    • chronic low intensity auditory hallucinations or delusional thoughts;
    • compulsive rituals which can be diverted;
    • low grade apprehensiveness, hypersensitivity, occasional panic;
    • vague or infrequent suicidal ideation;
    • rejection sensitivity and emptiness feelings;
    • low grade sad/helplessness;
    • persistent, negative self-talk;
    • persistent negative thoughts about life and future;
    • continuous urge for substance use/including caffeine, nicotine, sugar, etc.

    +Warning Signs/Symptoms of Relapse = subclinical symptoms with increasing intensity

    • sleep problems, appetite change, weight change, anhedonia;
    • trouble concentrating or making decisions;
    • social withdrawal and isolation;
    • vague feelings of unrealness or increasing sense of inner emptiness;
    • tenseness or nervousness;
    • cravings for substances;

Table 5.2 continues on page 97.

TABLE 5.2. *Continued*

- feeling too much energy, too talkative, racing thought;
- suspicious/fear of others;
- irritability, argumentativeness or temper;
- moodiness, discouragement, lowered energy;
- vague thoughts of self-harm or hurting others;
- feelings of worthlessness.

+Skills—Self-Management Skills

- personal hygiene and grooming;
- obtaining, handling and maintaining housing;
- using transportation system;
- food preparation skills;
- job finding/interviewing skills;
- job maintaining skills;
- obtaining and managing money;
- self-responsibility for one's actions.

+Skills—Relational Skills

- friendship and intimacy promoting behaviors;
- assertiveness communication;
- negotiation;
- problem solving;
- conflict resolution;
- identification and expression of feelings;
- modulation of impulses;
- modulation of cognitions;
- modulation of affects;
- capacity to cooperate and collaborate with others;
- empathy.

+Skills—Treatment Management Skills

- knowledge of medications, side effects and compliance strategies;
- ability to collaborate with treatment team and clinician;
- recognize and cope with persistent symptoms;
- recognize and manage warning symptoms.

admits to any suicidal ideation, no other "higher" level issues, such as the patient's social security disability application or lost welfare check, can be discussed until the "lower" or more basic treatment issue is reasonably resolved.

Medication Strategies

Psychotropic medications have been commonly used in the treatment of borderline patients both to reduce Axis I symptoms as well as modulate temperament/style dimensions. A full gamut of medications have been tried with this patient population: low dose neuroleptics, tricyclic antidepressants, anticonvulsants, and most recently, selective serotonin reuptake inhibitors. Given that the diagnosis of borderline personality disorder encompasses a heterogeneous group of patients often with intractable symptoms, both clinicians and patients have held high—and even magical—expectations for medication as a cure or at least a palliative. Nevertheless, while rational pharmacotherapeutic treatment of borderline pathology is unquestionably challenging, it can be quite rewarding for both clinician and patient (Silk, 1996).

The basic treatment strategy is to match a specific pharmacologic agent to a specific target symptoms and/or dimension of temperament. Recent pharmacological and neurobiological research suggests that the borderline disorder encompasses three treatment targets: affective instability, impulsive aggressivity, and cognitive distortion, including transient psychotic phenomenon (Coccaro & Kavoussi, 1991). Affective instability, impulsive aggressivity, and cognitive distortion also reflect basic dimension of temperament in many borderline patients.

It appears that affective instability is related to brain abnormalities in adrenergic and cholinergic systems. Agents like lithium carbonate and carbamezapines are effective in modulating affects. Abnormalities in central nervous system serotinergic function resulting in impulsivity seems to respond to serotonergic agents like Prozac. Finally, abnormalities in central dopaminergic systems may account for transient psychotic symptoms. Thus, low-dose neuroleptics have been shown to be effective with this symptom cluster.

The possible efficacy of serotonin reuptake inhibitors specifically with borderline pathology such as dysphoria and impulsive-aggressive behavior has been the subject of a number of clinical trials. Fluoxetine (Prozac) appears to be effective in treating symptoms related to depressed mood and impulsive aggressivity (Coccaro, 1993). There are some potential complications or disadvantages with pharmacotherapy in the treatment of borderline patients. First, is the matter of noncompliance either related to side effects or to secondary gain. Medications can serve as leverage to control the prescribing clinician or other caregivers. Demands for frequent changes in dosage or type of medication, overdosing, and failure to take the medication prescribed are all means of transference acting out. Second, borderline patients may appear to others to have improved from medication but report they feel worse, or vice versa. Gunderson (1989) suggested that this apparent paradox may ensue to the extent the patient believes that symptomatic improvement will result in undesirable consequences, such as loss or abandonment of dependent gratifications.

Schema Change Strategies

Once the borderline patient has achieved a sufficient measure of stability, it is then possible to address more traditional therapeutic issues. As noted earlier, schemas of abandonment/loss, unlovability/defectiveness, and dependence/incompetence are often seen in borderline patients. There are two general approaches to modifying such schemas. The more traditional is the psychodynamic approach in which the strategy is clarification, confrontation, interpretation, and working through. According to Masterson and Kleig (1990), therapeutic confrontation is the most effective psychodynamic tactic for working with borderline patients.

The other basic approach to modifying schemas is the cognitive therapy strategy. Layden et al. (1993) described the use of memory reconstruction, schema identification, imagery exercises, and the use of physical cues for modifying borderline schemas. Five extended case examples illustrate the cognitive therapy strategy of schema modification. Turner (1992) described an interesting integrative approach which he called dynamic–cognitive behavior therapy of the borderline personality disorder. In this approach, schemas are modified with both dynamic and cognitive therapy methods.

Group Treatment Strategies

The general consensus is that group therapy can be extremely effective with borderline disordered individuals. Group therapy has a number of advantages over individual therapy. Particularly noteworthy is that group tends to "dilute" intense transferences that otherwise would be directed to the individual clinician. Instead, affects like rage are diluted and directed toward other group members. Borderline patients also find it easier to accept feedback and confrontation from group peers than from an individual clinician. Groups also provide opportunities to understand and master such borderline defenses as splitting and projective identification.

There are some disadvantages and difficulties in treating borderline patients in groups. First, because of their propensity for acting out, these patients can be quite disruptive in traditional therapy groups consisting of high-functioning individuals. Second, they may feel deprived amidst the competition of other group members for the group leader's nurturance. Third, these patients may be easily scapegoated because of their primitive manner of expression. And they may maintain a certain distance in the group because of their privacy attachment to their individual psychotherapist. For that reason, borderline patients seem to fare better in homogeneous groups consisting of all or mostly borderline patients.

Behaviorally oriented groups for borderline patients focus less on intrapsychic and interpersonal dynamics and more on disordered patterns and symptomatic behavior. Accordingly, they are particularly suited for helping these patients acquire the specific skills necessary to control their affects, reduce their cognitive distortions and projective identifications, and find alternatives to self-destructive behaviors. Linehan (1993) provided a manual-guided strategy for the treatment of self-destructive behavior and impulsivity. Group sessions use didactic instruction, skill training, and behavioral rehearsal techniques. Some of these social skills training interventions, such as distress tolerance training and interpersonal skills training, are described in Chapter 3 of this book. These twice weekly sessions for 1 year are complemented with weekly individual counseling.

Research supports the clinical observation that these intervention strategies are remarkably effective (Linehan et al., 1991). Parasuicidal female borderline patients were randomly assigned to dialectical behavior therapy groups or to traditional community treatment. Those in the behavioral therapy groups had fewer incidents of parasuicide, and had significantly fewer inpatient psychiatric days compared with those in traditional treatment. They were also more likely to remain in individual therapy (Linehan et al., 1991).

Marital and Family Therapy Strategies

Parents and siblings of borderline patients have high incidence of affective disorders, alcoholism, antisocial personality disorder, and borderline personality disorder or traits. Usually, the parent–child relationship in borderline families is characterized by both neglect and overprotectiveness. Borderline families are also noted to display increased impulsivity, affective instability as well as significant problems with individuation, boundary violations, and enmeshment. Thus, involving the borderline patient's family or partner can be useful in decreasing enmeshment, respecting boundaries, and facilitating individuation. Family therapy can also increase overall family functioning and communication, and provide education about the nature of the disorder, while supporting compliance with medication or other treatment modalities. Family therapy can also be useful, and in some instances necessary, in maintaining borderline patients in outpatient psychotherapy. This is particularly the case when borderline patients remain financially and/or emotional dependent on their parents. To the extent that the family is motivated and has some capability of modulating affects and controlling projections, they may be a helpful adjunct to the overall treatment plan. Glick, Clarkin, and Goldsmith (1993) suggested that a mixture of systems, psychodynamic, behavioral, and psychoeducational family therapy intervention is preferable to a single approach to family therapy. Following are three different approaches for working with borderline patients in the context of their families.

Everett, Halperin, Volgy, and Wissler (1989) described a psychodynamically oriented approach with five specific treatment goals: increasing the family's ability to reduce the systemic splitting process; increasing family members' capacities for owning split-off objects and moving toward interacting with others as a "whole person"; reducing oppositional and stereotypic behavior of all family members; "resetting" external boundary for both unclear and intergenerational systems and internal boundary for spousal, parent–child, and sibling subtypes; and permitting a clearer alliance between the parents and limiting reciprocal intrusiveness of children and parents. Five treatment strategies for accomplishing these goals in an outpatient family treatment setting are developing and maintaining a therapeutic structure; reality testing in the family; interactional disengagement; intervening in the intergenerational system; and solidification of the marital alliance and sibling subsystem.

Solomon (1998) and Lachkar (1998) also described psychodynamically based treatments for troubled relations when one of the partners meets criteria for borderline personality disorder while the other meets criteria for narcissistic personality disorder. Both of these approaches emphasize the self-psychology perspective but recognize that systemic dynamics need to be considered.

A structural family approach is particularly useful for couples where the partner with borderline pathology is overly involved in the relationship while the other is distant and disengaged. Issues such as inclusion and rejection, nurturance and neglect, and symbiosis and abandonment become the basis for structurally rebalancing the couple subsystem within the larger family system (Sperry, 1995).

Relationship enhancement therapy is a potent psychoeducational intervention that has also been shown to be particularly useful in couples relationships when one partner has borderline pathology. Because borderline patients have major deficits in self-differentiation and communication, relationship enhancement's focus on skill building seems promising, particularly for mildly to moderately dysfunctional borderline patients. The clinician functions largely as a coach to develop the necessary relational skills in the course of 2-hour conjoint sessions (Waldo & Harman, 1993, 1998).

A history of childhood abuse can complicate efforts to use family modalities, especially if family members were party to the trauma. When the abuse has been particularly malevolent, family involvement probably should not be encouraged. However, if the trauma has been less malevolent family sessions may eventually be possible (Perry et al., 1990).

Combined and Integrative Treatment Strategy

There is growing consensus that combined treatment is essential for effective outcomes with the borderline personality disordered individual (Koenigsberg, 1993). This consensus reflects the severity of this condition and its apparent treatment resistance. Clincial experience suggests that there are clear differences between the prognosis and treatability of the high-functioning borderline individuals (i.e., GAF over 65) and the low-functioning borderline individuals(i.e., GAF below 45). Use of long-term psychoanalytically oriented psychotherapy may be possible with the highest functioning borderline individuals, but it is likely to be too regressive for lower functioning borderline individuals. In line with the basic premise of this book, the lower the patient's functioning and motivation and readiness for treatment, the greater the likelihood that treatment must be integrated and combined for it to be effective.

Combined treatment for borderline patients is indicated for those with severe symptoms for which symptom relief has been slow with psychosocial treatment, for those with overmodulated affects, for those with impulsive aggressivity, and for those with transient psychotic regression. These patients should have combined medication and individual therapy. Similarly, borderline patients with significant interpersonal disturbance and identity issues should be considered for combined medication, individual, and group treatment modalities. Furthermore, to increase medication compliance and to more accurately assess the effects of medication, conjoint treatment in which family sessions or sessions with a significant other, roommate, or job supervisor should also be considered.

Contraindications to combined treatment include a variety of patient presentations. Patients with high overdose potential who cannot be controlled with limit setting are probably not candidates for combined individual and medication treatment. Group treatment, including partial hospitalization, may be an alternative. Patients who may be responsive to medication but have a history of negative therapeutic reactions probably should not be offered individual psychotherapy. Similarly, patients who use medication to precipitate crises in therapy or where medication becomes the central focus of therapy probably should not be offered combined treatment (Koenigsberg, 1993).

Combining medication with individual therapy is the most common integrative modality. Kleig (1989) skillfully described the integration of pharmacotherapy within an individual psychotherapy context. He provided three guidelines for the effective use of medication: careful attention to diagnostic precision, evaluation of objective signs rather than subjective symptoms when determining when and which medication to use, and controlled awareness of the risks to therapeutic medication. Several case examples are provided that illustrate these guidelines.

A variety of transference phenomena can complicate combined treatment efforts with borderline patients. Patients with a history of transference enactments should probably be offered a trial of medication prior to the introduction of intensive individual psychotherapy to avoid or reduce such enactments. Otherwise, the clinician should consider using a structured medication management protocol in an individual format. Furthermore, issues of splitting are particularly common with borderline patients when medication is monitored by one clinician and psychotherapy is provided by another. However, splitting can also become manifest when the prescribing clinician also provides formal psychotherapy. In the case of two clinicians, when both clinicians are able to integrate psychological and biological perspectives and regularly collaborate with one another to present a "united front," splitting can be reduced or eliminated (Woodward, Duckworth, & Guthiel, 1993). When there is a single clinician, splitting is only possible when the clinician has a split view (i.e., biological vs. psychological) of treatment.

Further complicating matters is the task differential between medication prescribing and practicing psychotherapy. Whereas psychotherapy favors spontaneous discourse and activity on the part of the patient, medication monitoring is much more directive and requires considerable clinician activity. Because borderline patients may find it disruptive and difficult to move between these two tasks, it can be useful to set aside a few minutes at the beginning of a session to review medication effects and arrange for prescription, and then shift to the more obvious psychotherapeutic mode of discourse (Koenigsberg, 1993).

Medication compliance is often a problem in combined treatment with borderline patients, especially when medication is perceived by the patient as a chemical means by which the clinician can exert control over the patient's mind and will. Thus, medication compliance can be viewed as acquiescing to the control of the clinician, whereas noncompliance is viewed as taking back that control. For this reason, it is important for the clinician to elicit specific fantasies the patient has about medication and its effects, as well as the meaning of medicating the patient for the clinician in the countertransference (Koenigsberg, 1991). The interested reader is referred to Koenigsberg (1991, 1993) for a more detailed discussion of combined treatment issues with borderline patients.

Finally, combined treatment for lower functioning borderlines can be accomplished in a community-based setting. Usually, several treatment modalities will need to be combined. These often include individual therapy, group therapy, medication, drug and alcohol services, psychosocial rehabilitation, crisis intervention, and crisis housing. These modalities are often provided concurrently and usually are coordinated by a case manager (cf. Nehls & Diamond, 1993, for a detailed description of this strategy).

☐ Pattern Maintenance and Termination Strategies

Termination Issues

Termination can be extremely difficult and distressing for borderline patients. Because abandonment is an essential dynamic in borderline pathology, modifying the abandonment schema has to be the central focus of treatment. For this reason, it is essential that the treatment plan include provision for dealing with past interpersonal losses. Saying good-bye and grieving are skills most borderlines have never developed, and so therapy becomes the place where these skills and this corrective emotional experience usually begins. It must also deal with the anticipated loss of the current clinician(s) in the final phase of treatment. Losses need to be reframed as "necessary losses" and abandonment as "memories" that are treasured and not forgotten. Necessary losses are viewed as developmental opportunities to trade a secure, predictable experience and set of feelings for newer, growth opportunities that can only occur when an earlier experience is relinquished, but never really forgotten. In short, necessary losses and past memories are a prerequisite for personal growth and development.

Even in treating lower functioning and more severely disordered borderline patients who will require continued medication long after formal psychotherapy is completed, the matter of loss is still germane. Even though the patient may have quarterly medication monitoring sessions, the intensity of daily or weekly meetings with one or more clinicians no longer exits, and so it is perceived as a loss. Usually, the hypersensitivity that many borderline individuals experience with the anticipation of loss can be, in part, desensitized by weaning sessions. In longer term therapies, this may mean reducing the frequency of sessions from daily to weekly to biweekly to monthly and then even quarterly over the last year of a 2- to 3-year course of treatment, or for the last half or third of therapy for 1- to 2-year treatment courses. When only 12 to 20 sessions per year are possible, it may be possible to meet weekly for 5 to 10 sessions and then spread the remaining sessions out on a biweekly and then monthly basis for the remainder. Spacing out sessions allows patients to "contain" their abandonment fears. It also allows them the opportunity to use transitional objects and develop a sense of self-constancy between sessions, something they never would have believed was possible.

Finally, it is helpful for clinicians and borderline patients to collaboratively develop a plan of self-therapy and self-management following termination. It is recommended that these patients set aside an hour a week to engage in activities that continue the progress made in formal treatment. They might keep a diary or work on selected exercises. They could observe, monitor, and analyze obstacles and thoughts that interfered. Or, they might look ahead at the coming week and predict which situations could be troublesome, and plan ways to cope with feelings of loss or impulses to act outs. The goal of such effort is, of course, to maintain treatment gains and maintain the newly acquired pattern.

Relapse Prevention Strategies

Another essential aspect of the treatment plan and process is relapse prevention. Because borderline patients can easily revert to their maladaptive pattern, it is necessary to predict and plan for relapse. The final phase of treatment should largely focus on relapse prevention. An important goal of relapse prevention is predicting likely difficulties in the time period immediately following termination. Borderline patients need to be able to analyze specific external situations such as new individuals, unfamiliar places, as well as internal states such as specific avoidant beliefs and fears and other vulnerabilities that increase the likelihood of them responding with avoidant behavior in the face of predictable triggers. Once predicted, patients can develop a contingency plan to deal with these stressors. Clinicians may find it useful to have patients think and talk through the following questions: What can I do if I find myself resorting to my previous pattern? What should I do if I start believing my old beliefs more than my new beliefs? What should I do if I relapse?

A belief that is particularly troubling for borderline patients is, "I'll be alone forever. Everyone that I really need abandons me." This belief is easily activated and borderline individuals need to dispute it whenever it comes to mind. Furthermore, they need to anticipate the situations and circumstances when this belief is likely to arise and plan for it.

☐ Case Example

Tammy R. is a 25-year-old, single White woman with a 6-year history of inpatient and outpatient psychiatric treatment. Two weeks after she was married she experienced suicidal ideation and abandonment feelings that led to the first of six hospitalizations. This hospitalization appears to have been precipitated by her husband leaving her for an out-of-town meeting. Since then she has been in continuous treatment of one sort or another with four different therapists and three different psychiatrists. Her most recent therapist of 2 years has focused on a number of regressive issues, including early childhood emotional abuse, which probably accounts for the four hospitalizations during that time.

At the time of the current evaluation she complained of vague, occasional suicidal ideation, dysphoria, initial insomnia, and confusion about life and career goals. She was notably deficient in the skills of symptom management, interpersonal effectiveness, and self-management of affect regulation and impulse control. The skill deficit in affect regulation and impulse control were noted in her mood lability with chronic dysphoria and parasuicidality, which involved impulsive wrist-cutting, binge drinking, and overdosing with prescribed medications. She regularly used projective identification and splitting. Records show the patient had been functioning with a GAF in the mid-60s prior to her first admission but over the past 2½ years has fluctuated between 30 and 52. Currently, she is receiving Social Security Disability and is living alone in an apartment. She reports receiving regular morning phone calls from her mother asking "if I made it through the night without hurting myself."

Her developmental history included a chaotic family environment with an alcoholic father who reportedly left when the patient was 5 years old, and a mother who appears to be inconsistent but overly enmeshed with the patient even at the time of the evaluation. The patient was an honor student in high school, had particular difficulty maintaining friendships with female peers, and described a series of ill-fated relationships with boyfriends. She married right after high school and this relationship lasted 18 months before her husband left her "because of my crazy, clinging behavior." After high school, she had worked as a restaurant cashier while attending college. During the past 6 years, she has accumulated over 90 semester hours but had changed majors enough that it might require as much as 2 years to complete degree requirements.

Her medical history was noncontributory. She binges on wine and beer usually on weekend evenings when she is "lonely and mad that everyone else is going out and having fun." She had smoked marijuana in high school for a while but denies any current use of it or other substances, including various over-the-counter medications. She denied the use of nicotine and admitted that she consumes no more than the equivalent of two cups of coffee/caffeine a day. She has had trials of several antidepressants and neuroleptics. At the time of the evaluation, she was being prescribed Mellaril 75 mg HS and Zoloft 50 mg QD. Medication compliance appears to have been inconsistent, although compliance with therapy sessions—individual twice weekly—was relatively consistent. She indicated that she had been compliant with medication prior to her first overdose on it, and thereafter was ambivalent about filling prescriptions believing that if she had medications around her apartment she might be tempted to overdose again. At one point, family therapy had been suggested but her mother refused it and the matter was never broached again. The following treatment strategies were used with Tammy.

Engagement Process

Like many borderline disordered individuals, Tammy believed the purpose of therapy was for the therapist to take responsibility for making her feel better. However, because of her dependency needs, Tammy also needed to please her therapist. Thus, she had good attendance for partial hospital programs and appeared to collaborate with treatment. But she did not really collaborate. For example, she would "forget" to fill prescriptions and "misunderstand" how she was to keep a diary of her feelings, thoughts, and behaviors, and otherwise had difficulty taking responsibility for herself.

Turning to the matter of her expectations for treatment: When queried about her expectations, she indicated that even though she had tried individual therapy in the past, it did not seem to have worked for her. That somehow the treatment "just got stuck" and she was not sure that it really would be any different this time. Still, she recognized that she needed help and that she didn't believe she could make it without some kind of treatment.

Pattern Analysis

Her pattern was characterized by abandonment and dependency schemas and a dysregulated temperament. Her developmental history suggested that she wanted to be loved, taken care of, and directed. And, although she had attempted to individuate from her family, she was doubtful of her ability to function independently. An underlying belief—a core schema—was that if she functioned autonomously her mother, husband, or significant other would rebuke and abandon her. She learned that to obtain love she had be compliant and emotionally needy, whereas being self-reliant led to being reproached and abandoned. Although she wanted to be independent and make her own decisions, taking control of her life frightened her because she was unsure of what she would do with her life. Her struggle to establish a college major reflected this conflict. Consequently, she vacillated between submission and depression. Unfortunately, neither her early environment nor later life fostered the development of necessary self-regulation and relational skills. This, along with her maladaptive schemas of abandonment and dependency, led to her vulnerability toward acting out and self-harm as well as submissiveness and depression. Finally, it appears that actual or perceived rejection involving close relationships triggers this maladaptive pattern and her impulsive acting out. Diagnostically, she met criteria for major depressive episode, recurrent and borderline personality disorder with dependent and histrionic features. Figure 5.1 summarizes these style features.

Pattern Change

Because Tammy had essentially failed to respond to weekly individual therapy sessions in the past, it was unlikely that she would she would now, even if therapy was specifically directed toward modifying her maladaptive schemas. Her impulsive acting out suggested an unmodulated style or temperament, which needed to be addressed prior to schema issues. Regarding treatment modalities, her negative set about past treatment outcomes and her low expectations for the efficacy of current psychopharmacotherapy and psychotherapy in an individual format were sufficient to warrant a change in modality. Clearly, tailored, combined treatment was indicated.

Accordingly, she was referred to a partial hospital program with a focused treatment program for severe personality disordered patients. The 5-day-a-week programming attempted to achieve a holding environment in which participants could work at modulating troublesome affects, be-

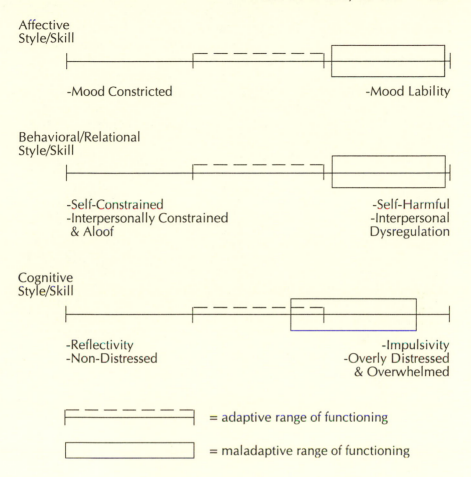

Affective
Style/Skill

-Mood Constricted   -Mood Lability

Behavioral/Relational
Style/Skill

-Self-Constrained   -Self-Harmful
-Interpersonally Constrained   -Interpersonal
 & Aloof   Dysregulation

Cognitive
Style/Skill

-Reflectivity   -Impulsivity
-Non-Distressed   -Overly Distressed
                                 & Overwhelmed

= adaptive range of functioning

= maladaptive range of functioning

FIGURE 5.1. Style/skill dimensions of borderline personality disorder.

haviors, and cognitions and reduce deficits in self-management and relational skills. It consisted of daily symptom management, distress tolerance, and social skill training groups, as well as weekly medication groups and individual therapy sessions that focused only on her progress in the program and on issues and concerns that Tammy was unable to discuss in group sessions. Twice-weekly occupational therapy and pre-employment training was also part of the programming. Tammy quickly responded to the consistency and stability of the program structure. Her binge drinking and fear of overdosing on prescribed medication subsided in the first 2 weeks. Thus, plans for substance abuse counseling were shelved. After 6 months in the program, Tammy's GAF was 60. She then moved to the partial hospital's aftercare program for approximately 12 months. It consisted of twice-weekly programming involving occupational training, a relapse-prevention group, as well as individual and group therapy sessions that focused on her abandonment and dependency schemas. During this time, three family evaluation sessions were held with Tammy and her mother to foster more functional boundaries between mother and daughter. Even though she was somewhat reluctant, Tammy's mother agreed that it would be more helpful for Tammy the adult to make phone contact with her at least once a week instead of mother's usual daily wake-up call. These efforts appear to have successful.

Tammy's patterns were interpreted as learned patterns rather than immutable traits and thus they could be changed through self-observation, cognitive restructuring, and skill training. Medication was considered to be an essential component of treatment because of her dysphoria and insomnia. It was felt that combined medication and group treatment could probably replace the negative set she had toward medication. Therefore, she was begun in a medication group in the partial hospital program that emphasized symptom management training for persistent symptoms. For Tammy, these included chronic dysphoria and parasuicidality. Over time, Mellaril (which had been prescribed for the insomnia) was replaced by Desyrel, and the SSRI, Zoloft, was increased to 100 mg. It was hoped that in addition to stabilizing mood, the increased dose of the SSRI would reduce impulsivity (Siever & Davis, 1991; Silk, 1996), but it did not. Thus, more reliance was placed on impulse control training in skill training groups. Later, medication was monitored in individual outpatient sessions.

Pattern Maintenance and Termination

Not surprisingly, termination issues for Tammy involved abandonment fears. After completing 18 months in the partial hospitalization and aftercare program, she continued with monthly individual sessions that included medication monitoring. It is anticipated that after 1 year, these monthly sessions will be decreased to quarterly sessions. Because much of her individual and group therapy was directed toward the abandonment schema and because the intensity of treatment has been weaned from daily to monthly, Tammy will be reasonably desensitized to rejection/abandonment.

In establishing a plan for preventing relapse, it is necessary to target the situations and circumstances in the patient's pattern that triggered relapse. Tammy was most vulnerable to relapse on weekend nights when she was lonely and angry and felt abandoned by others and had access to alcohol. The plan Tammy developed in her relapse prevention group included arranging to have a planned activity scheduled for weekends, even if it was just going out to a movie by herself, and not keeping alcohol in her apartment.

After 12 months, she was able to return to college classes full time, work part time at a low-stress retail sales job, and continue in a twice-weekly relationship skills group and a monthly medication group. Seven months later, her GAF was estimated at 70 when she was "graduated" to monthly individual therapy sessions including medication monitor. She graduated from college a year later and began working full-time as an elementary school teacher. Although she dates occasionally, she has no plans for remarrying. She has established gratifying friendships with two other teachers at her school, and has been able to set and maintain limits on phone calls from her mother. As noted above, she will probably continue on medication indefinitely with quarterly follow up. Finally, no hospitalizations nor suicide gestures were reported since the tailored treatment began some 3 years ago.

☐ Summary

Effective treatment of the borderline personality disordered patients requires the establishment of a collaborative therapeutic relationship fostered by focal treatment interventions to modify the maladaptive pattern and then to maintain the more adaptive pattern. Borderline disordered patients have considerable difficulty focusing on the patient–clinician relationship to the extent necessary to work within a traditional individual psychotherapeutic mode. Usually, it is not until they experience some degree of modulation of their affective, behavioral, and cognitive styles that they are amenable to modifying or changing their character structure. Thus, an integrative and combined approach, usually including medication, can be effective in treating even symptomatic, lower functioning borderline patients. Table 5.3 summarizes the treatment intervention strategies most likely to be effective with this disorder.

TABLE 5.3.   Treatment Interventions with Borderline Personality
Disorder

Phase	Issue	Strategy/Tactic
Engagement	Patient's difficulty viewing clinician as helpful/collaborative	Confrontation and limit-setting; Treatment contract and "holding environment"
Transference	Dependency, merger fantasy	Set limits, confront, interpret
Countertransference	Anger, rescue fantasies	Monitor
Pattern Analysis	**Triggers:** personal goals, close relations	
Pattern Change	**Treatment Goal:** increase stability and cohesiveness	
Schemas/Character	Abandonment/loss schema Unlovability/defective schema, Dependency/ incompetence schema	Interpretation strategy, Schema changing strategy
Style/Temperament		
a. Affective Style	Overmodulated affects	Emotional awareness and regulation training
	Impulse dyscontrol	Impulse control training
b. Behavioral/ Relational Style	Self-mutilation and parasuicidality	Self-management training
	Interpersonal deficits and vulnerability	Interpersonal skill training
c. Cognitive Style	Overmodulated thinking and projective identification	Cognitive awareness training
	Distress intolerance	Distress tolerance training
Maintenance/ Termination	Abandonment fears, relapse proneness	

Dependent Personality Disorder

Dependent personality disorder is recognized by its pervasive pattern of dependency and submissive behavior. Even though it is considered more amenable to treatment than the borderline or narcissistic personality disorders, effective treatment of dependent personalities involves a number of unique therapeutic challenges. As in the rest of this book, this chapter describes a number of specific strategies for effectively managing and treating this disorder with regard to engagement, pattern analysis, pattern change, and pattern maintenance. In addition to individual psychotherapeutic strategies and tactics, group, marital and family, medication, and integrative and combined treatment strategies are detailed. An extensive case example illustrates the treatment process. Before turning to treatment strategies, the DSM-IV description and criteria are briefly presented.

☐ DSM-IV Description and Criteria

DSM-IV offers the following description and criteria of dependent personality disorder:

TABLE 1. DSM-IV Description and Criteria for Dependent Personality
Disorder

301.6 Dependent Personality Disorder

"A pervasive and excessive need to be taken care of that leads to submissive and clinging behavior and fears of separation, beginning by early
adulthood and present in a variety of contexts, as indicated by five (or
more) of the following:

(1) has difficulty making everyday decisions without an excessive amount
of advice and reassurance from others

(2) needs others to assume responsibility for most major areas of his or her
life

(3) has difficulty expressing disagreement with others because of fear of
loss of support or approval. (Note: Do not include realistic fears of
retribution.)

(4) has difficulty initiating projects or doing things on his or her own
(because of a lack of self-confidence in judgment or abilities rather
than to a lack of motivation or energy)

(5) goes to excessive lengths to obtain nurturance and support from others,
to the point of volunteering to do things that are unpleasant

(6) feels uncomfortable or helpless when alone, because of exaggerated
fears of being unable to care for himself or herself

(7) urgently seeks another relationship as a source of care and support
when a close relationship ends

(8) is unrealistically preoccupied with fears of being left to take care of
himself or herself"

Reprinted with permission from the *Diagnostic and Statistical Manual of Mental Disorders*, Fourth
Edition. Copyright 1994, American Psychiatric Association.

☐ Engagement Strategies

Early Session Behavior

In early sessions, especially the first, dependent personality disordered individuals typically wait for the clinician to begin the conversation. After
the clinician inquires about the reason for coming to the sessions, these

patients can present an adequate description of their current situation. But, then are likely to become silent. Predictable comments include, "I'm not sure what to say. I've never been in therapy before," or "Ask me something, then I'll know how to answer your question." When the clinician asks other questions, the cycle tends to be repeated.

Nevertheless, interviewing these individuals and establishing rapport can be relatively easy and enjoyable. After experiencing some initial anxiety, these patients can quickly establish a bond of trust with the clinician. For this reason, patients with dependent personalities are among the easiest of the personality disorders to engage in the therapeutic process. Presuming the clinician provides pleasant advice and support, as well as being empathic in the face of their indecisiveness and failures, the interview will flow smoothly. Yet, as the clinician moves to explore the detriments of their submissiveness, these patients predictably become noticeably uncomfortable—particularly in the early phase of treatment. If the dependency isn't pursued with an empathic ear, these individuals may change to another clinician. But if pursued empathically, these individuals are likely to cooperate and meet their clinician's expectations. They can be expected to respond to questions and to clarify and elaborate. They can also tolerate abrupt transitions and will allow deep feelings to be probed. However, they do not easily tolerate confrontation and interpretation of their dependency needs and behaviors (Othmer & Othmer, 1994).

Facilitating Collaboration

Unlike treatment with most other personality disorders, collaboration can be achieved or at least approximated rather early in the course of treatment of the dependent personality disorder. Largely, because of their strong needs to please and be accepted by others (particularly authority figures) dependent personality disordered patients are likely to be quite willing to respond favorably with the expectations and demands of clinicians. Thus, they will, more likely than not, collaborate with psychotherapeutic and medication regimens if the clinician requests and expects collaboration. However, because they have an equally strong propensity to enlist others in taking care of and making decisions for them, dependent patients may not really want to assume the degree of responsibility that real therapeutic collaboration requires. So they may be passively compliant and take prescribed medications as directed, but not actively follow through on other treatment matters that were "mutually agreed" on, nor initiate self-responsible behaviors unless reminded by the clinician. In other words, compliance is much easier than collaboration for dependent patients, and both patients and clinicians may mistake compliance for collaboration. Clearly, the distinction between the two must be pointed out, and the transference issue underlying it must be dealt with (Sperry, 1995).

Transference and Countertransference

Predictable transference and countertransference problems are noted to arise in treating dependent personality disordered individuals. Perhaps the most common transference involves patients' efforts to engage clinicians in assuming responsibility for all their personal decisions. Unfortunately, this transference can provoke a countertransference in which clinicians succumb to these efforts either because they feel exasperated by patients' protestation of their inadequacy or because of their wish to be idealized. These responses not only reinforce over-reliance on clinicians but also their belief that they really don't have to become independent nor self-sufficient. Another transference involves patients' failure to make progress in treatment, while maintaining their attachment to clinicians. So, as noted above, they may passively respond to the clinical directive but not take initiative or become truly active in the treatment process. Unfortunately, as noted earlier, this compliant attitude may be mistaken for collaboration with treatment goals. The countertransference involved here is the clinician's failure to confront the lack of actual change and unwitting reinforcement of the patient's refusal to be responsible and become more self-reliant. A final transference involves the sheer number of requests for advice, nurturance, and guidance that these patients make early in the course of treatment. The clinician's efforts to modulate these requests—which are essentially demands—early in treatment to prevent the patient from becoming overly disappointed and possibly result in premature termination. This transference invites the clinician's countertransference response of emotional withdrawal, which subsequently reinforces the patient's neurotic guilt about their neediness (Perry, 1995).

Generally speaking, it is useful for the clinician to make aspects of the patient's dependent transference explicit. Although an open discussion of the patient's dependency needs may not always be appropriate very early in treatment, this discussion is both useful and necessary after a working relationship has been established. Timing of the feedback is important. Typically, such feedback is best communicated in the context of the situation that has arisen wherein the patient's dependent behaviors have been problematic.

☐ Pattern Analysis Strategies

Pattern analysis with borderline disordered individuals involves an accurate diagnostic and clinical evaluation of schemas, styles, and triggering stressors as well as their level of functioning and readiness for therapeutic change. Knowledge of the optimal *DSM-IV* diagnostic criterion along with the maladaptive pattern of the borderline personality disordered individual is not only useful in specifying diagnosis but also in planning treatment that is tailored to the patient's unique style, needs, and circumstances. The optimal criterion specified for the dependent personality disorder is that the patient needs others to assume responsibility for most major areas of his or her life (Allnutt & Links, 1996). This reliance on others serves to alleviate anxiety around making decisions while maintaining a subservient posture in the relationship. With this criterion in mind, the clinician can plan and direct treatment to focus on these deficits in self-confidence and overreliance on others.

Pattern refers to the predictable and consistent style and manner in which a patient thinks, feels, acts, copes, and defends the self. Pattern analysis involves both the triggers and response—the "what"—as well as a clinical formulation or explanatory statement—the "why"—about the pattern of a given borderline patient. Obviously, such a clinical formulation specifies the particular schemas and temperamental styles unique to a given individual rather than the more general clinical formulation that will be noted here.

Triggers

Generally speaking, the "triggers" or "triggering" situations for dependent patients are stressors related to self-reliance and being alone. This means that when dependent disordered individuals are engaging in behaviors, discussing, or even thinking about being alone or relying on their own resources and become distressed their disordered or maladaptive pattern is likely to be triggered and their characteristic symptomatic affects, behaviors and cognitions are likely to be experienced or exhibited. For instance, the thought "I hate to be alone" triggers anxious, panicky feelings and the likelihood of giving up their own aspirations and goals to cling to another for guidance (Othmer & Othmer, 1994).

Schemas

Generally speaking, the underlying schemas of dependent disordered individuals involve a self-view of weakness, defectiveness, and inadequacy. Their world view is that others will protect and care for them (Sperry & Mosak, 1996). Among the most frequently encountered schemas in dependent patients are functional dependency/incompetence and failure to achieve. The *dependency/incompetence schema* refers to the core set of beliefs that one is incapable of handling daily responsibilities competently and independently, and so must rely on us to make decisions and initiate new tasks. *Failure to achieve* refers to the core set of beliefs that one cannot perform as well as others so no attempt is made out of fear of failure (Bricker, Young, & Flanagan, 1993; Young, 1990).

Style/Temperament

There are three style/temperaments that may need to be addressed in formulating treatment with the dependent personality: affective, behavioral–interpersonal, and cognitive. Needless to say, these styles exacerbate and are exacerbated by their schemas. Dependent individuals are prone to overmodulated anxiety. Their cognitive style is one of uncritical cognitive appraisal and the naive perception of others' capacity and desire to care for them. Cloninger (1987) noted that their behavioral response style is characterized by harm avoidance. As such, they are considerably inhibited and are unlikely to show initiative or to function independently. Accordingly, they tend to be limited in assertiveness and deficient in the problem-solving skills like planning, decision making, and implementing decisions, and other self-management skills related to independent functioning. Relationally, they have been so consistently overreliant on others and thus need to please others that they have not developed adequate skills in assertive communication nor in negotiation nor conflict resolution.

☐ Pattern Change Strategies

In general, the long-range goal of psychotherapy with a dependent personality is to increase the individual's sense of independence and ability to function interdependently. At other times, the clinician may need to settle for a more modest goal. That is, helping the individual become a "healthier" dependent personality. Treatment strategies typically include challenging the individual's convictions or dysfunctional beliefs about personal inadequacy, and learning ways in which to increase assertiveness. A variety of intervention strategies are useful in achieving these goals.

After the maladaptive pattern has been identified and analyzed in terms of schemas and style and skill deficits, the therapeutic process involves relinquishing that pattern and replacing it with a more adaptive pattern. Thus, the pattern change process involves modifying schemas, modulating style dysregulations, and reversing skill deficits. The process of modifying the maladaptive schemas of dependent personality disordered patients usually follows efforts to modify style and skill-deficit dimensions because schema change early in the course of treatment is often resisted by the patient.

Schema Change

The functional dependency/incompetence and failure to achieve schemas are supported by such injunctive beliefs as, "I'm helpless when I'm left alone," "Somebody must be around at all times to help me do what I need to do or in case something goes wrong," "I must not do anything that offends my supporters and helpers," and, particularly, "I can't make decisions on my own" (Beck, Freeman, & Associates, 1990). In the schema change process, the clinician and patient work collaboratively to understand the developmental roots of the maladaptive schemas. Then these schemas are tested through predictive experiments, guided observation, and re-enactment of early schema-related incidents. Finally, dependent patients are directed to begin to notice and remember counterschema data about themselves and their social experiences.

Style/Temperament Change

Unlike borderline personality disorder and narcissistic personality disorder in which temperaments are markedly overmodulated in all three style dimensions of affective, behavioral/relational, and cognitive, the dependent personality disorder does not display as much dysregulation. Nevertheless, skill-training interventions are quite effective in modulating styles and reversing skill deficits.

Anxiety dysregulation can be modulated with the graded exposure strategy that is a core feature of anxiety management training. Assertive communication training and problem solving training are useful in reducing dependent patients' harm avoidance and inhibition and thereby increase their capacity to function more energetically and independently. This training also reduces their skill deficits problem solving, particularly decision-making. Cognitive awareness training and pinpointing and challenging automatic beliefs can be helpful in redirecting their cognitive style marked by naive, uncritical appraisal.

Medication Strategies

Dependent personality disordered individuals often exhibit Axis I diagnoses, particularly anxiety and depressive disorders. Such a concurrent anxiety or depressive disorder can be treated with a variety of psychotropic agents. However, if medication is not warranted for an Axis I disorder, caution should be exercised in prescribing medication for the Axis II dependent personality disorder. It has been observed that dependent patients have a tendency to become habituated to anxiolytics; and antidepressants are not recommended for reactive symptoms in dependent individuals (Reid, 1989).

Group Treatment Strategies

Group treatment can be particularly effective with dependent personality disordered individuals. In deciding if group treatment should be extended, and if it is, two factors need to be considered. The first involves the patient's motivation and potential for growth. If it is reasonably high, a more interactional psychotherapy group may be indicated. This type of group provides a therapeutic milieu for exploring the inappropriateness of passive-dependent behavior and for experimenting with greater assertiveness (Yalom, 1985). On the other hand, if dependent traits reflect severe personality impairment and/or the absence of prosocial behavior (such as assertive communication, decision making, and negotiation on ongoing supportive problem-solving groups) or a social skills training group might be indicated. The second involves whether the group should be homogeneous—treatment targeted at dependency issues shared by all group members—or heterogeneous wherein group members have different personality styles or disorders. Clinical lore suggests that dependent patients tend to get "lost" in heterogenous groups, whereas time-limited assertiveness training groups that are homogenous and have clearly defined goals have been shown to be very effective (Lazarus, 1981).

Marital and Family Therapy Strategies

There is a very limited literature on family therapy interventions involving individuals with the dependent personality. Clinical experience suggests that dependent personality disordered individuals are brought to family therapy by their parents. These individuals are frequently older adolescents or young adults between the ages of 20 and 35 who present with a neurotic or psychotic symptom. Changing the enmeshed family relationship tends to be anxiety provoking for all parties, and thus, there is considerable resistance from other family members when only one member of the family is in therapy (Harbir, 1981).

Similarly, there is relatively little literature on marital therapy with dependent personality disordered individuals. Clinical experience suggests that a dependent partner can function adequately if their marital partner consistently meets their needs, but he or she often becomes symptomatic and impaired when the marital partner's support is withdrawn or withheld. Accordingly, it is useful to engage the cooperation of the marital partner in treatment because of the negative impact on the relationship as the dependent partner becomes less anxious and more independent, and because treatment progress results when the marital partner is also committed to the treatment goals (Sperry, 1995).

Nurse (1998) described the marital dynamics between a partner who meets criteria for dependent personality disorder and a partner who meets criteria for narcissistic personality disorder. He also offered an interesting approach to planning treatment based on the Millon Multiaxial Clinical Inventory (MCMI-III). This approach to treatment emphasizes the use of feeding back MCMI-III data to the couple, communication training, and homework assignments.

Barlow and Waddell (1985) described a 10-session couples group intervention for the treatment of agoraphobia where the symptomatic partner exhibits dependent personality features. This intervention encourages the nonsymptomatic partners to function in a coaching role collaborating on treatment goals, which effectively discouraged the role of reinforcing their partner's agoraphobia and dependency. Over the course of this group treatment, panic and agoraphobia symptoms remit while the marital relationship shifts from dependency to interdependency.

Combined and Integrative Treatment Strategies

Barlow and Waddell's (1985) effort to combine behavior therapy in a group setting with dependent couples is one of many examples combining modalities with dependent personality disordered individuals. However, there is relatively little research published on integrative treatment strategies with dependent patients. Nevertheless, there have been some case reports of efforts to use anxiety reducing strategies in both dynamic and cognitive therapies (Sperry, 1995).

One such example was reported by Glantz and Goisman (1990). They described their effort to integrate relaxation techniques within psychodynamic psychotherapy with dependent patients. A controlled breathing and progressive muscle relaxation strategy was used to merge split self-representations in the course of exploration psychotherapy. The strategy was introduced after signs of split self-representation had been identified. Patients practiced the strategy and were prescribed it as homework. When they achieved an adequate level of relaxation in the session they were asked for visual images of both conflicting self-representations. After clear images were elicited and discussed, they were instructed to merge the images. The results of this strategy were noteworthy in that most dependent patients responded with improved interpersonal relationships.

☐ Pattern Maintenance and Termination Strategies

Termination Issues

Termination can be very difficult for dependent patients, because termination represents relinquishing an important, necessary relationship with a nurturing, caretaking figure. Recall that dependent patients erroneously view independence as being totally alone and without the support of anyone, while dependence means being totally cared for and supported. Not surprisingly, termination can be particularly anxiety producing for dependent patients. Consequently, the clinician must endeavor to minimize the negative effects of termination, and frame termination as a therapeutic intervention in and of itself. Three therapeutic strategies can facilitate treatment termination with the dependent patient. First, termination will be made easier if the clinician makes it clear that termination does not require a permanent break in the therapeutic relationship. However, the clinician does not want to send a mixed message, indicating that the patient is ready to terminate but is not "really" terminating. Rather, the clinician must frame the termination in a manner that emphasizes the patient's successful work during treatment (Bornstein, 1993, 1994).

Second, the clinician should offer the predictive interpretation that dependency needs may complicate the termination process. Conveying this prediction to the patient in a matter-of-fact, nonjudgmental fashion can simultaneously preempt the patient's conscious or unconscious wish to subvert termination and continue therapy indefinitely, and provide the patient with useful feedback regarding the ways in which dependency strivings can adversely affect other important interpersonal relationships.

Third, spacing out sessions allows patients to become more independent of the clinician and the treatment process. In this process of becoming less reliant on the clinician's direct support during weekly sessions, they learn to rely more on their own resources as well as develop or maintain other support systems. As they become increasingly able to tolerate this separation, their maladaptive dependency pattern shifts to a more adaptive and healthier pattern of interdependence. A variant of spacing sessions is to set a specific termination date at the very outset of treatment. Mann (1973) described this option for higher functioning individuals with relatively focal issues, including dependency, for the 12-session dynamically oriented treatment he called "time-limited psychotherapy." With higher functioning dependent personality disordered patients, it is possible to set a specific termination date and then focus treatment on increasing self-reliance; however, clinical experience indicates that considerably more than 12 sessions are needed.

If they would continue to be prescribed medication, they might slowly shift to scheduled medication monitoring appointments at 3- to 6-month intervals. If they were not receiving, or have already been weaned from, medication they might have booster sessions scheduled at 3-, 6-, or 12-months intervals.

Finally, it is helpful for clinicians and dependent patients to collaboratively develop a plan of self-therapy and self-management following termination. It is recommended that these patients set aside an hour a week to engage in activities that continue the progress made in formal treatment. They might work on selected exercises. They might look ahead at the coming week and predict which situations could be troublesome and plan ways to cope with dependent behaviors. The goal of such effort is, of course, to maintain treatment gains and maintain the newly acquired pattern.

Relapse Prevention Strategies

Another essential aspect of the treatment plan and process is relapse prevention. Because dependent patients can easily revert to their previous avoidant pattern, it is necessary to predict and plan for relapse. The final phase of treatment should largely focus on relapse prevention. An important goal of relapse prevention is predicting likely difficulties in the time period immediately following termination. The patient needs to be able to analyze specific external situations such as new individuals, unfamiliar places, as well as internal states, such as specific avoidant beliefs and fears and other vulnerabilities that increase the likelihood of responding with avoidant behavior in the face of predictable triggers. Once predicted, patients can develop a contingency plan to deal with these stressors. Clinicians may find it useful to have patients think and talk through the following questions: What can I do if I find myself resorting to dependent patterns? What should I do if I start believing my old dependency beliefs more than my new beliefs? What should I do if I relapse?

A belief that is particularly troubling for dependent patients is, "I can't stand being alone." This belief is typically activated when dependent patients face situations that require self-reliance or being alone. In such instances, it can be helpful for patients to imagine what their clinician might have them think and do in such a circumstance. With this imaginal strategy, the patient will no longer feel totally alone nor feel that they must be totally self-reliant.

☐ Case Example

Janet R., the 29-year-old mother of a 4-year-old daughter, experienced her first panic attack while on a business trip with her husband. Sweating, difficulty breathing, numbness and tingling of the extremities, and chest pain convinced her that she was having a heart attack. She was quickly transported to a local emergency room, where physical examination ruled out a myocardial infarction. After intramuscular Valium partially relieved her symptoms, the trip was aborted and she returned home. In the subsequent week, her sleep and anxiety improved to some extent. But because she had experienced anxiety episodes of increasing severity and had begun to avoid crowded places and shopping malls over the previous 2 years, she readily accepted her family physician's psychiatric referral.

Engagement Process

Before ending their initial session, the psychiatrist asked her to keep a daily log of the sensations, events, thoughts, and feelings associated with each episode of anxiety and what she did about it. The expectation was that accomplishing this task would not only provide Janet a sense of control, but also assess her readiness and capacity for treatment. One week later, she reported moderate improvement in symptoms: no panic attacks, decreased anticipatory anxiety, less fitful sleep, and better concentration.

Pattern Analysis

The psychiatric evaluation elicited a family history of treatment for anxiety, and depression in her mother. Recent stressors included having few friends because they had just moved from another city, her daughter's starting kindergarten, and anticipatory anxiety about the recent business trip. She was unable to tell her husband she was frightened of accompanying him, and felt guilty when the trip had to be rescheduled because of her panic attack. Needless to say, she had considerable difficulty expressing negative feelings, particularly toward authority figures, including her husband. She met *DSM-IV* criteria for panic disorder with agoraphobia and dependent personality disorder.

As a child she recalled being reprimanded whenever she directly expressed her feelings: From an early age, as the oldest child, she assumed many parental duties because of her mother's long-term psychiatric hospitalizations. As a result, she had little opportunity to develop an identity distinct from that of looking after others. She believes she is inadequate as a parent, wife, and person. Similarly, she believes that she needs others not only to survive but to be happy. In addition to the core schema of dependency/incompetence that is typical of the dependent personality disorder, Janet also internalized the self-sacrifice schema. Furthermore, she uses the defenses of denial and suppression to cope with anger. These defenses underlie her maladaptive pattern, which was to refrain from expressing her needs, avoid confronting others to garner their support and avoid their rejection, as well as to enlist others in making decisions for her. She has noticeable skill deficits in assertiveness and anxiety modulation. Figure 6.1 summarizes these style features.

Pattern Change

In the second session the psychiatrist then prescribed relaxation training to help Janet regulate her psychological and physiologic arousal and an antidepressant to block panic attacks and her anticipatory anxiety. Between sessions she has considerable difficulty with the controlled breathing exercises and rather than deep breathing she instead hyperventilates.

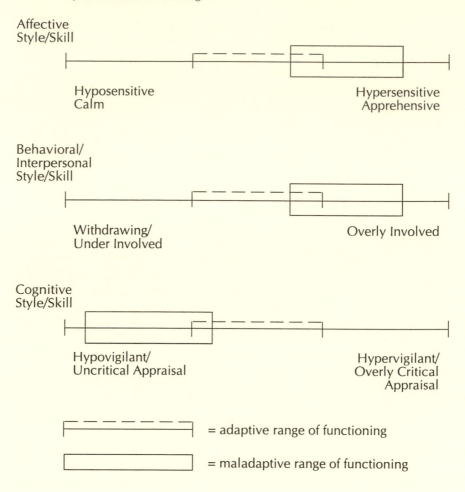

FIGURE 6.1. Style/skill dimensions of dependent personality disorder.

Fearful she will have another panic attack, she abandons the exercise. Subsequently, adjunctive group treatment is discussed in the third session. With some hesitation, Janet agrees to participate in an 8-session anxiety modification group in addition to biweekly individual sessions with the psychiatrist.

The group sessions emphasized relaxation and assertive communication. By the fourth session, she had few symptoms but was still fearful of a panic attack. Needless to say, she continued to depend on the antidepressant to "keep me safe and secure." Her response to the assertiveness training was equivocal. For example, she had been able to refuse a request to coordinate a school event, yet she still could not stand up to her husband and felt guilty when she contemplated confronting him about his burdensome demands. Janet and her group therapist collaboratively developed a desensitization program for her phobic avoidance. She developed a hierarchy of fear-provoking activities and situations, and then used her new relaxation skills to avert anxiety in each activity and situation. She was able to begin shopping in relatively uncrowded stores and dining out during off-peak hours. During the last group session, Janet developed a relapse prevention plan.

Meanwhile, in individual sessions, the psychiatrist helped Janet explore her dependency/self-sacrificing schema. During the 6th session, Janet recognized the intensity of her anger and became more anxious for several weeks. But in the 11th session, she reported a new confidence having been able to cope principally by relying on her ability to control symptoms with relaxation rather than on medication alone. By now the antidepressant was changed from daily dose to an as needed or prn dose. In the 13th session she indicated that she thought she needed to stop treatment, citing expense and her new-found confidence. The psychiatrist hypothesized that she had been frightened by a glimpse of her anger at her parents and her husband, but she rejected this interpretation. She said that despite her husband's appreciation of her symptomatic improvement, he seemed annoyed by what he perceives as her growing reliance on treatment, but he refused a conjoint session to discuss the matter. The clinician acceded to her request to stop treatment but emphasized his availability should she wish to explore further the psychological predisposition of her illness.

Two months later, Janet returned to treatment in dismay. Her anxiety had recurred following news of her sister's impending divorce. There had been continuous phone calls at all hours of the day and night. Janet had to frequently interrupt her daily responsibilities "to be available to my sister in her time of need." Janet's husband, who up to this point had been supportive, was becoming exasperated. In 12 further individual sessions spread out over 5 months, Janet explored these conflicts and the underlying schemas of dependence/incompetence and self-sacrifice in a focal dynamic psychotherapy mode. Her objective was to understand that she was identifying with the psychiatrist's caretaking role to the detriment of both her sister's needs and her own. Was this not a familiar pattern? And was this behavior not alienating her husband, the one person who was receptive to her needs? The transference interpretation struck home. She advised her sister to seek psychiatric treatment. With her husband's help, she set limits on her sister's intrusion. Janet identified how her compliance with the clinician's statements was, in fact, a defense against her rage when he did not gratify her dependency needs.

Pattern Maintenance and Termination

By the 25th individual session, she was relatively symptom-free. More important, she understood how to manage her emotions and personal relationships. The earlier conceived relapse plan was reviewed and revised. Fully active again, Helen terminated treatment. Follow-up consisted of participation in an assertiveness-training group in which she functioned as the group facilitator. In the ensuing months, she rarely used the antidepressants she had been given. One year later, she reported an increased capacity to deal with anxiety and her concerns about self-sufficiency. She continued to practice assertive communication and relaxation. To her surprise, she noted the beneficial effect of her new insight and competence with her husband and family members.

☐ Summary

Effective treatment of dependent personality disordered patients requires the establishment of a trusting patient–clinician relationship fostered by focal treatment interventions to modify the maladaptive pattern and then maintain the new pattern. Higher functioning dependent patients may be reasonably adaptive and functional at work and socially, and thus may be able to profit from single modality treatment. However, many dependent patients have concurrent symptom disorders in addition to their personality disorder and are much less adaptive and functional. These patients have considerable difficulty making progress in traditional individual psychotherapy. Thus, an integrative and combined approach, which may include medication, can be effective in treating the majority of dependent personality disordered patients. Table 6.2 summarizes the treatment intervention strategies most likely to be effective with this disorder.

TABLE 6.2. Treatment Interventions with Dependent Personality
Disorder

Phase	Issue	Strategy/Tactic
Engagement	Silent demand for clinician to make decisions and solve their problems; Comply rather than collaborate	Allow measured amount of dependence at first; Gradually introduce collaboration theme; Distinguish collaboration from compliance
Transference	Clinging resistance; Multiple requests; Idealize clinician	Set clear limits on clinician–patient relationship; Frustrate patient's dependency fantasies by refusing to collude
Countertransference	Rescue fantasies; Directive role; Failure to confront patient's limited progress	Monitor own thoughts/ feelings regarding rescue/directive role; Confront patient's limited progress
Pattern Analysis	**Triggers:** Self-reliance and being alone	
Pattern Change	**Treatment Goal:** Autonomy with interdependency/ healthier dependence	
Schema/Character	Dependency/incompetence schema; Failure to achieve schema	Interpretation strategy
Style/Temperament		
a. Cognitive Style	Naive, uncritical cognitive appraisal	Pinpoint/challenge automatic thoughts

Table 6.2 continues on page 130.

TABLE 6.2. *Continued*

Phase	Issue	Strategy/Tactic
b. Emotional Style	Anxiety dysregulation	Anxiety management training; Graded exposure
c. Behavioral/ Relational	Assertiveness training; Problem solving training; Involve significant others in treatment process	
Maintenance/ Termination	Fear of termination/ abandonment with paradoxical worsening of progress	Predictive interpretation; Weaning/ spacing out sessions; Time-limited format with target termination date; Scheduled booster session

Narcissistic Personality Disorder

The Narcissistic Personality Disorder has become increasingly recognizable as a diagnostic entity in the western world. At the same time the definition and determinants of this disorder have been carefully articulated. For instance, Masterson (1993), among others, has differentiated two versions of the disorder: the "exhibitionistic" narcissistic personality disorder and the "closet" narcissistic personality disorder. The more common version, the exhibitionistic or grandiose form of this disorder, is specified in DSM-IV. The treatment of both versions of this disorder involves a number of unique therapeutic challenges. Nevertheless, these individuals can be effectively treated. This chapter describes specific engagement, pattern analysis, pattern change, and pattern maintenance and termination strategies for effectively managing and treating the grandiose form of this disorder. In addition to individual psychotherapeutic strategies and tactics, group, marital and family, medication, and integrative and combined treatment strategies are detailed. An extensive case example illustrates the treatment process. Before turning to treatment strategies, the DSM-IV description and criteria are briefly presented.

☐ DSM-IV Description and Criteria

According to DSM-IV, the narcissistic personality disorder is described as a pervasive pattern of grandiosity (in fantasy or behavior), need for admiration, and lack of empathy, beginning by early adulthood and present in a variety of contexts. It is indicated by at least five of the following nine criteria listed in Table 7.1.

TABLE 7.1.   DSM-IV Description and Criteria for Narcissistic Personality Disorder

---

301.81 Narcissistic Personality Disorder

"A pervasive pattern of grandiosity (in fantasy or behavior), need for admiration, and lack of empathy, beginning by early adulthood and present in a variety of contexts, as indicated by five (or more) of the following:

(1)   has a grandiose sense of self-importance (e.g., exaggerates achievements and talents, expects to be recognized as superior without commensurate achievements)

(2)   is preoccupied with fantasies of unlimited success, power, brilliance, beauty, or ideal love

(3)   believes that he or she is "special" and unique and can only be understood by, or should associate with, other special or high-status people (or institutions)

(4)   requires excessive admiration

(5)   has a sense of entitlement, i.e., unreasonable expectations of especially favorable treatment or automatic compliance with his or her expectations

(6)   is interpersonally exploitative, i.e., takes advantage of others to achieve his or her own ends

(7)   lacks empathy: is unwilling to recognize or identify with the feelings and needs of others

(8)   is often envious of others or believes that others are envious of him or her

(9)   shows arrogant, haughty behaviors or attitudes"

Reprinted with permission from the *Diagnostic and Statistical Manual of Mental Disorders*, Fourth Edition. Copyright 1994, American Psychiatric Association.

☐ Engagement Strategies

Early Session Behavior

Effectively interviewing narcissistic individuals requires considerable ability to recognize, understand, and respond to their unique dynamics. Throughout the interview, they give the distinct impression that the interview has only one purpose: to underscore their self-promoted importance (Othmer & Othmer, 1994). These individuals often present themselves as self-assured, pretentious, and entitled to having their needs met, and they appear indifferent to the clinician's perspective. Typically, they are unwilling to conform to expectations associated with the "patient" role but have well-defined expectations for the clinician's role. They expect clinicians to mirror or reflect their specialness, and will respond by idealizing them—at least temporarily—as wonderful clinicians and human beings. However, should a clinician confront their grandiosity early in the treatment process, they will inevitably respond with rage and possibly terminate treatment prematurely. Not surprisingly, narcissistic individuals prefer open-ended questions that permit them extended descriptions of their many talents, accomplishments, and future plans.

Narcissistic patients may present for treatment in pain following a narcissistic injury. They want and expect that the clinician will soothe this wrenching pain. When the clinician fails to recognize the need for or fails to provide sufficient soothing the patient is likely to react angrily or leave treatment. Not surprisingly, rapport and engagement into the treatment process occurs only after a considerable period of mirroring and soothing. One of the reasons the establishment of rapport and engagement is so difficult is because of clinician countertransference. Clinicians can easily become bored, exasperated, and even angry in the initial interviews as they try to listen attentively to the patient's monologue of self-promotion. If the clinician can remain patient through this period and sufficiently mirror the patient, engagement can be achieved and the formal work of confronting and interpreting their grandiosity can begin.

Facilitating Collaboration

Developing a collaborative relationship with narcissistic patients can be extraordinarily challenging. The notion of collaboration is distasteful to them because collaboration implies some measure of equality, and they have a vested interest in maintaining their sense of superiority over everyone, including clinicians. Rather than view treatment as a collaborative endeavor, narcissistic individuals are more likely to perceive it as a competitive endeavor in which they fight to establish and maintain their position of superiority. Not surprisingly, they will avoid, derail, or deride the clinician's efforts to directly influence them to collaborate. Furthermore, these individuals have usually had limited experience in cooperative interactions and very likely have skill deficits in this cooperation and collaboration. Accordingly, the clinician does well to mirror these individuals, "join" with their grandiosity, and not act out on their countertransference during the early period of treatment. Once the clinician passes this therapeutic test, the patient is less likely to view the clinician as a competitor. Then, the clinician will be more likely to convey to the patient that both might be able to work together in the best interest of the patient.

Transference and Countertransference

Common transferences involve idealization, devaluation, and projective identification. Narcissistic patients typically idealize clinicians when they provide patients mirroring and other emotional supplies, but they can quickly shift to devaluing clinicians when they are confronted or emotional supplies are withheld. Similarly, in projective identification the patient excludes the clinician just as she was once excluded by her own parents. An aspect of the patient is projected onto the clinician who identifies with that self before helping the patient to reintroject it (Gabbard, 1994).

Four countertransferences that can be activitated in working with narcissistic patients are described by Gabbard (1994). The first, failure of clinicians to recognize their own narcissistic needs, may be operative as early as the initial session. The narcissistic patient may idealize his current clinician while devaluing previous clinicians. Rather than viewing this as a defensive maneuver, the clinician who longs for idealization may uncritically believe that she has unique talents that were lacking in the patient's previous providers. Another countertransference is boredom that can arise when the patient appears to be oblivious to the clinician's presence. When clinicians must endure serving as a sound board function for narcissistic patients for long periods of a session, they may easily experience boredom and subsequently respond critically or by not mirroring. In addition, clinicians may also struggle with feelings of being controlled by narcissistic patients. This occurs when patients interpret the clinician's body language and paralanguage as indicators of the clinician's rejection or boredom, resulting in the clinician feeling coerced into focusing entirely on their every movement. Gabbard (1994) suggested saying something like:

"It seems to hurt your feelings when I clear my throat or fidget in my seat because you feel I am not giving you my full attention" (p. 520). Finally, clinicians may have to contend with countertransference feelings, such as anger, hurt, or feeling impotent, in response to patient's devaluing comments of them.

☐ Pattern Analysis Strategies

Pattern analysis with narcissistic disordered individuals involves an accurate diagnostic and clinical evaluation of schemas, styles, and triggering stressors as well as level of functioning and readiness for therapeutic change. Knowledge of the optimal DSM-IV criterion along with the maladaptive pattern of the narcissistic disordered individual is not only useful in specifying diagnosis but also in planning treatment that is tailored to the narcissistic patient's unique style, needs, and circumstances. The optimal criterion specified for the narcissistic personality disorder is that the patient has a grandiose sense of self-importance (Allnutt & Links, 1996). Both planned treatment goals and interventions should reflect this theme of grandiosity and specialness.

Pattern refers to the predictable and consistent style and manner in which a patient thinks, feels, acts, copes and defend the self. Pattern analysis involves both the triggers and response—the "what"—as well as an explanatory statement—the "why"—about the pattern of a given narcissistic patient. Obviously, such a clinical formulation specifies the *particular* schemas and temperamental styles unique to a given individual rather than the more *general* clinical formulation that will be noted here.

Triggers

Generally speaking the "triggers" or "triggering" situations for narcissistic individuals involve evaluations of self. This means that when narcissistic disordered individuals are engaging in behaviors, discussing, or even thinking about being alone or relying on their own resources and become distressed, their disordered pattern is likely to be triggered and their characteristic symptomatic affects, behaviors, and cognitions are likely to be experienced or exhibited. For instance, an actual or perceived threat to the "I'm the only one that counts" can trigger rageful thoughts and affects, along with lowered self-esteem, and compensatory self-centered and even retaliatory behavior.

Schemas

Generally speaking, the underlying schemas involve a self-view of grandiosity, specialness, and entitlement, and a view of the world that demands special treatment and dispensation from the rules and regulations that govern others (Sperry & Mosak, 1996). Among the most frequently encountered schema in narcissistic patients is the entitlement/self-centeredness schema. Occasionally, the insufficient self-control/self-discipline schema or abuse/mistrust also is observed. The entitlement/self-centeredness schema refers to the core set of beliefs that one is entitled to take or receive whatever is wanted irrespective of the cost to others or society. The insufficient self-control/self-discipline schema refers to the core set of beliefs that one has such limited control and ability to tolerate frustration that achieving goals or controlling impulses and emotional outbursts is unlikely. The abuse/mistrust schema is noted in the hypervigilant and suspicious narcissist. This schema refers to the core set of beliefs that others will hurt, humiliate, or take advantage of one (Bricker, Young, & Flanagan, 1993; Young, 1994).

Style/Temperament

There are three style or temperament dimensions that may need to be addressed in formulating treatment with the narcissistic personality: affective, behavioral–relational, and cognitive. Needless to say, these styles exacerbate and are exacerbated by their schemas. Narcissistic individuals are prone to overmodulated anger to the point of ragefulness. Behaviorally, they tend to be manipulative, whereas relationally they are likely to have difficulty relating to others except in a superficial manner. In addition, they tend to have significant empathic deficits. Finally, their cognitive style is marked by the capacity for cognitive distortion and projective identification. When impulsivity is also present, it further exacerbates the other style dysregulations. The most notable skill deficit in this disorder is the skill of empathic responding. Other skill deficits that may be present include negotiation and conflict resolution.

☐ Pattern Change Strategies

In general, the long-range goal of treatment with narcissistic personality disordered individuals is to increase their capacity and willingness to share and identify with others. Treatment strategies typically include challenging the individual's dysfunctional beliefs about specialness and grandiosity and learning to become more empathic.

After the maladaptive pattern has been identified and analyzed in terms of schemas, style and skill deficits, the therapeutic process involves relinquishing that pattern and replacing it with a more adaptive pattern. Thus, the pattern change process involves modifying schemas, and style-skill dimensions. The process of modifying the maladaptive schemas of narcissistic personality disordered patients usually follows efforts to modify style and skill-deficit dimensions because schema change efforts early in the course of treatment are usually resisted by the patient.

Schema Change

The entitlement/self-centeredness schema is supported by such injunctive beliefs as "It's essential that I get others' admiration, praise, and recognition," "Others should satisfy my needs," "I'm not bound by the rules that apply to others," "Others have no right to criticize me," and, particularly, "Because I'm so superior, I'm entitled to special privileges and treatment" (Beck, Freeman, & Associates, 1990). In the schema change process, the clinician and patient work collaboratively to understand the developmental roots of the maladaptive schemas. Then these schemas are tested through predictive experiments, guided observation, and reenactment of early schema-related incidents. Finally, narcissistic patients are directed to begin to notice and remember counterschema data about themselves and their social experiences.

Modification of the entitlement schema does not mean these individuals become selfless and no longer believe themselves to have special talents or capacity to influence and control others. It means that while they continue to view themselves with some degree of specialness, they are able to use their talents and capacities to influence others more for the common good rather than their own personal gratification.

Style/Temperament Change

Because narcissistic individuals tend to cognitively distort and overuse the defenses of splitting and projective identification, cognitive awareness training can be quite useful. With regard to emotional style wherein narcissistic rage is prominent, anger management training can be an effective intervention strategy. Because empathic deficits greatly affect relational style, empathy training and increasing intimacy promoting behavior is indicated. And, because impatience and impulsivity often exacerbate other style dysregulation, impulse control training may be necessary. As noted below, medication may also be a useful adjunct in modulating these style dimensions.

Medication Strategies

Narcissistic personality disordered individuals often exhibit Axis I diagnoses, including anxiety disorders and somataform symptoms. However, depressive disorders are the most common. When appropriate, these comorbid disorders can be treated with anxiolytic or antidepressant agents. Occasionally, these agents will also impact Axis II features. For instance, monoamine oxidase inhibitors and benzodiazepines can be a useful adjunct to skill training for the treatment of narcissistic rage. Occasionally, the use of antidepressants from the selective serotonin reuptake inhibitor class, such as fluoxetine or sertraline, will also reduce some of the impulsiveness and interpersonal sensitivity and reactivity noted in narcissistic individuals. The less their impulsivity, the more likely they will be able to control their ragefulness and projective identifications. However, most of the time, temperament or style dysregulations can only effectively be modulated with skill training.

Group Treatment Strategies

Group treatment has a role in the treatment of narcissistically disordered individuals. Alonso (1992) contended that group therapy is as effective as individual modes in treatment of narcissistic personality. Nevertheless, recent developments in conjoint marital therapy suggest that group treatment may have fewer indications than individual and couples therapy (Sperry, 1995).

Nevertheless, several factors contribute to the effectiveness of group treatment with these patients. First of all, peer rather than clinician feedback tends to be more acceptable to the individual. Second, transferences—particularly negative transferences—tend to be less intense in group compared with individual therapy. Working through intense effects is facilitated in groups because of the increased potential for positive attachments within the group and because of peer-group scrutiny of the individual's disavowed affects. Third, a group provides narcissistic individuals with sources of mirroring, objects for idealization, and opportunities for peer relationships. Finally, the group provides ready-made opportunities for narcissistic individuals to increase their ability to empathize with others, and to enhance both self-esteem and self-cohesion.

Not surprisingly, narcissistic patients can make unreasonable demands for attention in group treatment. These demands can be very taxing for other group members, particularly in heterogeneous groups. Accordingly, it is advisable to begin narcissistic patients in individual therapy as preparation for entrance into group treatment. Even though narcissistic pathology can strain efforts to achieve group cohesion, a properly run group can function as a container for splitting and projective processes. Nevertheless, the dropout rate for narcissistic personality disordered individuals is higher in long-term ongoing groups than in time-limited groups. Accordingly, concurrent individual psychotherapy that focuses on helping individuals to remain in group therapy is often useful.

Horowitz (1987) outlined the following four indications and contraindications for group treatment of narcissistic individuals: the presence of demandingness, egocentrism, social isolation and withdrawal, and socially deviant behavior. While these traits may be taxing to both clinician and group members, Horowitz contended that patients with such traits tend to be quite responsive to group treatment. Finally, attending to the unique needs of the narcissistic individual usually means that the clinician will place less emphasis on interpreting overall group dynamics and more on individual dynamics as they affect the group process (Sperry, 1995).

Marital and Family Therapy Strategies

Early reports on the use of family therapy with narcissistic personality disorder patients emphasized the treatment of adolescents in families with severe narcissistic pathology, wherein the adolescent was the identified patient on whom family members projected their own devalued view of themselves. More recent applications of family therapy to narcissistic personality disorder emphasize treatment of the entire family system from a systemic perspective (Jones, 1987).

Much has been published about marital therapy with the narcissistic spouse or couple. Solomon (1989, 1998) described a conjoint treatment strategy for narcissistic partners from a self-psychology perspective. Conjoint sessions are structured to functions as a "holding environment" for the distorted projections and other conflictual manifestations in the relationship. The therapist's empathic self is the basic tool of this kind of psychodynamic treatment.

Kalojera and his colleagues (Kalojera, Jacobson, Hoffman, et al., 1998) described an integrative blending of self-psychology and the systemic approach to the narcissistic couple that is noteworthy. Lachkar (1998) offered a number of clinically useful considerations for the treatment of couples where one partner meets criteria for narcissistic personality disorder while the other meets criteria for borderline personality disorder. This type of couple is increasingly common today. Nurse (1998) described the dynamics and treatment strategies for another common variant of the narcissistic couple: One partner meets criteria for narcissistic personality disorder while the other meets criteria for dependent personality disorder.

Relationship enhancement therapy has also been adapted to couples therapy with narcissistic spouses (Snyder, 1994). This approach emphasizes the learning and application of four basic interpersonal skills: (a) effective expression, (b) empathy, (c) discussion—mode switching between empathic and expresser roles, and (d) problem solving/conflict resolution. The clinician's role is to explain, demonstrate, and coach each skill in the conjoint session, whereas the partner's role is to practice these skills during and between sessions with progressively difficult issues. It should not be surprising that empathic skills and the subjective aspect of the expresser skill are notably deficient in narcissistically vulnerable couples. The clinician provides a "holding environment" in which narcissistic vulnerability is experienced and addressed productively rather than acted out. This results in both partners learning to express feelings with less risk of shame, while increasing their capacity to empathize with their partner (Snyder, 1994).

Combined and Integrative Treatment Strategies

There is seldom a single treatment strategy, such as mirroring or empathy training, that can ensure positive treatment outcomes with narcissistically disordered individuals. Rather, depending on the individual's overall level of functioning, temperamental patterns, defensive style, and skill deficits, a focused, specific, and sequentially coordinated tailored treatment protocol is usually necessary to accomplish treatment goals and objectives in a timely manner and fashion. As noted earlier, higher functioning individuals who meet either DSM-IV or dynamic criteria for a personality disorder have fewer troubling temperamental patterns, skill deficits, and defensive styles than the lower functioning individual. Consequently, the higher the functioning and the fewer skill deficits, the less likely a combined approach is necessary; whereas the lower the functioning and the more skill deficits/temperament dysregulation, the more an integrative, tailored and combined approach is necessary. This section describes such integrative and combined strategies.

Generally speaking, the psychodynamic approaches have largely emphasized the interpretation of narcissistic vulnerability regarding grandiosity and entitlement and soothing and mirroring frustrations to reduce narcissistic rage. The cognitive approaches have focused on modifying narcissistic vulnerability, emphasizing modification of schemas, moderating narcissistic expectations, and reducing cognitive distortions, particularly projective identification. The behavioral and psychoeducational approaches have emphasized skill training, particularly empathy training. Combining all three of these modalities is relatively easy to implement and quite acceptable to patients (Sperry, 1995). The usual time sequence for using these modalities is as follows: Begin with mirroring and mirroring interpretations to engage the patient in treatment. Next focus on reducing skill deficits and temperament dysregulation that would otherwise hinder the treatment process. This may include medication but almost always involves skill training, particularly empathy training (Snyder, 1994). This training can be accomplished in individual, group, or couples sessions. Then continue with the schema change strategy and other interpretation strategies. The case example that follows illustrates this sequencing of modalities.

☐ Pattern Maintenance and Termination Strategies

Termination Issues

Planned termination is usually not particularly difficult for narcissistic patients. Rather, for the reasons described in the *engagement* section, narcissistic patients tend to be premature terminators. There are some who, because of the clinician's early confrontative stance or failure to mirror sufficiently, experience treatment as another narcissistic injury and leave at the outset. But for all narcissistic patients, the therapeutic challenge is to engage these patients in the treatment process long enough to achieve basic treatment objectives. To that end, it may be necessary to conceptualize the treatment process as a series of discrete phases and establish treatment contracts for these phases. The initial phase usually involves resolution of distress. Many narcissistic individuals present for treatment with such sufficient distress that they will remain until it has lessened. For instance, they come for treatment because of depression, a serious narcissistic injury, or because of the distress they have created in the lives of others, such as a spouse who threatens divorce if treatment is not sought. These individuals will likely remain in treatment until they have achieved sufficient soothing or amelioration of their anxiety or depressive symptoms. Many of them terminate after experiencing relief of their distress. Accordingly, it is advisable to establish a treatment agreement for a given number of sessions focused on distress resolution and then re-evaluate and re-negotiate another series of sessions to focus on more general concerns. Needless to say, the clinician's challenge is to sufficiently "join" with the patient's entitlement so that the patient comes to believe that therapeutic change is in his or her best interest. The following case example illustrates these points.

Relapse Prevention Strategies

Relapse prevention is essential in the effective treatment of narcissistic individuals. Even though effective treatment greatly reduces their interpersonal sensitivity and narcissistic vulnerability, these individuals are still prone to narcissistic injury. The final phase of treatment should therefore emphasize relapse prevention. An important goal of relapse prevention is predicting likely difficulties in the time period immediately following termination. The patient needs to be able to analyze specific factors such as persons, places, circumstances, as well as specific narcissistic beliefs that can trigger their maladaptive pattern. Once predicted, patients can develop a contingency plan to deal with these stressors.

☐ Case Example

James K. is a 49-year-old, married chairman of the department of plastic and reconstructive surgery at a university school of medicine. He grudgingly came for psychotherapy because of depressive symptoms and because of ultimatums from his wife and boss. His wife demanded that he get help or she would divorce him. He had been married for 7 years to his current wife, and prior to that was married for approximately 5 years during the last 2 years of medical school and the first 3 years of his surgical residency. Recently his wife complained that she would no longer tolerate his constant need for attention nor his increasing rage and verbal abuse, which consisted of blaming, insults, and name calling. Lately, their time together was marked by either destructive conflict or cold distancing for days to weeks. In addition, the dean of the medical school had also warned him if he didn't adopt a "more consultive management style" he would be removed as chair of his department. Apparently, Dr. K. had increasingly alienated a number of his faculty over the past few years by his arrogant, demanding style and because he had recently fired two junior faculty for insubordination. The university grievance committee that reviewed the firings found that due process was not followed and recommended that the two faculty be reinstated. Dr. K. was furious with the committee's recommendation and demanded that the dean ignore it. It was then that the dean gave him the ultimatum. Dr. K.'s rage turned to depression manifested by dysphoria, insomnia, some anhedonia, and loss of energy. Although he had refused his wife's demand for couples therapy, he reluctantly agreed to individual psychotherapy.

Engagement Process

Like many narcissistic personality disordered individuals who enter treatment, Dr. K. was deeply narcissistically wounded and mildly to moderately depressed. Nevertheless, they usually seek treatment with great reluctance and demand that it be on their terms. Dr. K. announced during the first session that he was there against his better judgment and that he had no problems except for a wife who was a "bedeviling shrew" and a boss who was a "wimpish idiot." Reluctantly, he admitted that he was embarrassed and hurt by recent events particularly at the medical school but said these would pass. Mainly, he was concerned about his depressive symptoms, which were worsening over the past 3 weeks. He wanted an antidepressant. By the second session, his sleep was normalizing and he was more energetic but still was quite wounded. He responded to the clinician's mirroring and attentiveness and agreed to return for a third session. The clinician was a member of the school's psychiatry faculty and had responded to an emergency that resulted in being about 6 minutes late for Dr. K's third appointment. Dr. K. immediately launched into an attack on the clinician's character and competence, and stated he should never have trusted himself to the care of a junior faculty member, when he should have been seen by the chair of the department or at least a faculty psychiatrist who was listed in *Best Doctors in America*. The clinician successfully soothed Dr. K. and apologized for the delay. Later that session, Dr. K. announced his depression had lifted and he would no longer need treatment. The clinician offered a mirroring interpretation and suggested it might still be in Dr. K.'s best interest to consider some alternative ways of dealing with his wife, colleagues, and dean that would ease the current situation and prevent their recurrence. Dr. K. agreed it was in his best interest to "do some damage control" and committed to eight additional sessions after which the treatment contract would be reviewed.

Pattern Analysis

Although he did not meet criteria for major depressive disorder he did meet criteria for minor depressive disorder as well as narcissistic personality disorder. A review of his early childhood and later developmental history as well as his early recollections indicated a self-view of specialness and a world view in which others were to cater to his needs. His maladaptive pattern involved increasing self-aggrandizement, manipulation, and demands of others whenever he felt the slightest discomfort or lack of others' recognition. When criticized or otherwise narcissistically wounded he would engage in projective identification and ragefulness. This pattern reflects the maladaptive schema of entitlement/self-centeredness and, to some extent, the schema of insufficient self-control/self-discipline. This pattern also reflects style/skill deficits in accurate attributions, impulse control, and empathic communication. Figure 7.1 summarizes these style features.

Pattern Change

The eight sessions were arranged to include four individual weekly sessions and four weekly conjoint sessions. The individual sessions focused on cognitive awareness training and impulse control training skills. Even though he had previously refused couples therapy, Dr. K. was receptive to the conjoint sessions because the focus would be limited to interpersonal skills. Dr. K. agreed that the purpose of these sessions was to give him "another set of people skills" that he could "use when it was expedient." After all, he was proud of his persona of toughness and arrogance and didn't want to give it up. Empathy training exercises were the focus of four such conjoint sessions. In these sessions, both spouses were helped to understand their narcissistic vulnerability, expectations, and needs underlying their narcissistic defense. The clinician modeled empathic listening as well as empathic responding for them, and coached them in both listening and responding from the others' frame of reference. In part this was accomplished by role playing and role reversal in which Dr. and Mrs. K. played themselves expressing their feelings and concerns and then reversed roles. They agreed to practice these skills at least 30 minutes per day.

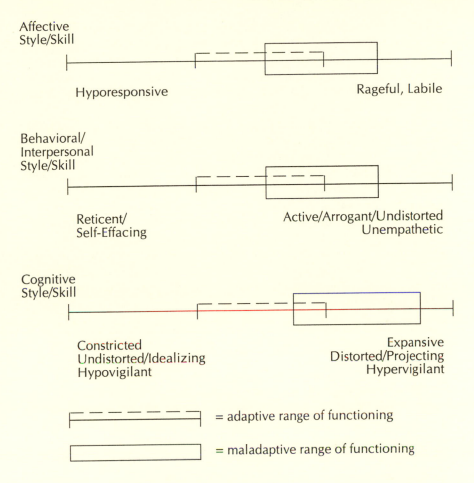

FIGURE 7.1. Style/skill dimensions of narcissistic personality disorder.

During the last of the four individual sessions, the eight-session treatment agreement was reviewed. The focal intensity of the individual and conjoint sessions, as well as their daily skill practice, resulted in a significant shift in the K.s' relationship. It had become much more respecting and caring, and they had been able to handle the few conflicts that had arisen in a more adaptive fashion. Dr. K. was also pleased that his work relationships were also less charged and he congratulated himself for "reinventing myself" by which he meant he now had a "good guy persona" too. Through mirroring interpretations, the clinician set the stage for discussing a continuation of the treatment contract. The modality would be individual psychotherapy, with a focus on further enhancement of the skills and understanding of self that had already been started. Not surprisingly, Dr. K. declined the invitation saying he had gotten what he had come for and was fine. The clinician offered to resume treatment if and when Dr. K. might find it beneficial.

Approximately 5 months later, Dr. K. was back in treatment. Two weeks earlier, following a stormy confrontation with him, Mrs. K. had filed for divorce. Dr. K. was crushed. He was dysphoric and panicky at the prospect of losing "the jewel of my life." Furthermore, he had begun experiencing palpitations that diagnosed as a cardiac arrhythmia for which medication was prescribed. He was agreeable to anything now, even couples therapy. Individual psychotherapy was begun with a focus on maladaptive schemas. The antidepressant was reintroduced for a short time until depressive and anxiety symptoms were ameliorated and then weaned. Twice weekly sessions were scheduled. These sessions continued for the next 11 months, after which they were reduced to weekly sessions for an additional 3 months.

Pattern Maintenance and Termination

During the course of this treatment period, Mrs. K. dropped the divorce action. A planned termination ensued. He had developed considerable insight into his need for specialness and control along with concomitant changes in his behavior. Dr. K. did not believe a scheduled follow-up appointment was necessary but agreed to call the clinician in 6 months. At that time, he reported that things were going reasonably well at work and even better at home. His son and daughter-in-law who had gotten married just after he started the long-term therapy had just visited and had brought their infant daughter. He and Mrs. K. were quite excited by the prospect of being grandparents.

☐ Summary

Effective treatment of narcissistic personality disordered patients requires the establishment of a trusting patient–clinician relationship fostered by focal treatment interventions to modify the maladaptive pattern and then maintain the new pattern. Because these patients may have considerable difficulty engaging in and profiting from traditional psychotherapy, an integrative-combined approach, which focuses on characterological, temperament, and skill dimensions may be essential for effective treatment outcomes. The case example illustrates the common challenges that these patients present, and the kind of clinician flexibility, resourcefulness, and level of competence required. Table 7.2 summarizes the treatment intervention strategies most likely to be effective with this disorder.

TABLE 7.2. Treatment Interventions with Narcissistic Personality Disorder

Phase	Issue	Strategy/Tactic
Engagement	Demanding mirroring; Easily narcissistically wounded	Mirroring; Minimize
Transference	Idealizing to devaluating; Projective identification	Mirroring interpretation
Countertransference	Not recognizing one's own narcissistic needs; Boredom; Feeling controlled by the patient; Angry, hurt, impotent	Monitor and interpret
Pattern Analysis	**Trigger:** evaluation of self	
Pattern Change	**Treatment Goal:** increased awareness and responsiveness to others' needs	
Schema/Character	Entitlement/self-centeredness; Insufficient self-control/self-discipline; Abuse/mistrust	Interpretation or schema change strategy
Style/Temperament		
a. Affective Style	Narcissistic rage	Anger management
b. Behavioral/Relational Style	Empathic deficits	Empathy training

Table 7.3 continues on page 148.

TABLE 7.2. *Continued*

Phase	Issue	Strategy/Tactic
c. Cognitive Style	Cognitive distortion; Projective identification; Hypervigilance	Cognitive awareness training Sensitivity reduction training
Maintenance/ Termination	Premature termination	"Join" patient's entitlement

8

CHAPTER

Histrionic Personality Disorder

The histrionic personality disorder as delineated by DSM-IV is not synonymous with the hysterical personality disorder described in the psychoanalytic literature. Rather the description and criteria of the histrionic personality disorder reflect a more primitive entity than the higher functioning hysterical personality. Needless to say, the treatment of the histrionic personality disorder is more challenging than the treatment of the hysterical personality. Nevertheless, these histrionic personality disordered individuals can be effectively treated. This chapter describes specific engagement, pattern analysis, pattern change, and pattern maintenance and termination strategies for effectively managing and treating this disorder. In addition to individual psychotherapeutic strategies and tactics, group, marital and family, medication, and integrative and combined treatment strategies are detailed. An extensive case example illustrates the treatment process. Before turning to treatment strategies, the DSM-IV description and criteria are briefly presented.

☐ DSM-IV Description and Criteria

DSM-IV offers this description and criteria for histrionic personality disorder:

149

TABLE 8.1. DSM-IV Description and Criteria for Histrionic Personality
Disorder

301.50 Histrionic Personality Disorder

"A pervasive pattern of excessive emotionality and attention seeking,
beginning by early adulthood and present in a variety of contexts, as
indicated by five (or more) of the following:

(1) is uncomfortable in situations in which he or she is not the center of
     attention

(2) interaction with others is often characterized by inappropriate sexually
     seductive or provocative behavior

(3) displays rapidly shifting and shallow expression of emotions

(4) consistently uses physical appearance to draw attention to self

(5) has a style of speech that is excessively impressionistic and lacking in
     detail

(6) shows self-dramatization, theatricality, and exaggerated expression of
     emotion

(7) is suggestible, i.e., easily influenced by others or circumstances

(8) considers relationships to be more intimate than they actually are"

Reprinted with permission from the *Diagnostic and Statistical Manual of Mental Disorders*, Fourth
Edition. Copyright 1994, American Psychiatric Association.

☐ Engagement Strategies

Early Session Behavior

Interviewing histrionic individuals is usually enjoyable, but it is always
quite challenging. The challenge is that these individuals are more interested in admiration and approval than in establishing a therapeutic relationship. The clinician can expect exaggerated emotionality, vagueness,
and superficiality in the first session. Histrionic females are likely to be
flirtatious, obsequious, or playful with a male clinician, whereas they are
more likely to engage in a power struggle with a female clinician (Sperry,
1995). Eliciting sufficient history and information to complete the diag-

nostic evaluation usually requires the clinician to neutralize the histrionic individual's vagueness, dramatics, or control. The clinician's use of open-ended and unstructured questions should be limited or avoided because these patients easily become sidetracked. Rather, it is more productive to pursue a basic theme, such as interpersonal conflict or a work issue, and then elicit specific examples while curbing their ramblings and contradictions. Confronting their contradictions may result in hostility and even loss of rapport, and thus it is preferable to express empathy and understanding. It should be anticipated that when they experience that empathy and understanding diminishing, they will return to vagueness or dramatization (Othmer & Othmer, 1994).

Because histrionic patients tend to regard the self as a recipient of the actions of others rather than as an agent of action, they report symptoms as caused or represented outside of the self. Accordingly, by repetitions and structured questioning the clinician can begin assisting these patients to clarify their experience, to provide everyday labels for them, and to recognize that thoughts and feelings come from within the self (Horowitz, 1995).

Facilitating Collaboration

Establishing a collaborative relationship with histrionic patients is somewhat similar to establishing such a relationship with dependent personality disordered patients. At the outset of treatment, both types of patients are likely to view clinicians as all-powerful rescuers who will make everything better for them. And, because of their global, impressionistic cognitive style and sense of specialness, histrionic patients tend to believe and expect that clinicians will somehow intuitively be able to appreciate and understand their needs and concerns without any or much intrapsychic exploration of these needs and concerns. For this reason it is essential that the clinician assume an active role at the outset of treatment. The more this active role is evidenced, the quicker the fantasy of the all-powerful rescuer will fade.

Histrionic patients must undergo a socialization process in which they experience the phenomenon of collaboration, which is quite foreign to them. Whenever histrionic patients beg and demand that they be helped or rescued, clinicians use questioning to assist them in arriving at their own solutions. Furthermore, clinicians must reinforce every instance of assertive and competence behaviors manifest in the early phase of treatment, rather than helping–demanding behaviors. The cognitive therapy strategy of guided discovery in which clinicians work with patients to understand the connection between patients' thoughts, images, feelings, and behaviors is particularly effective in facilitating collaboration with histrionic patients (Beck, Freeman, & Associates, 1990).

Transference and Countertransference

Two common transferences noted with histrionic patients are rescue fantasy and the erotic or erotized transferences. When histrionic patients bring a series of problems to clinicians expecting quick solutions, or otherwise feign helplessness, it is easy for clinicians to respond to their rescue fantasy by assuming an all-powerful/messianic or rescuer role. In the role of rescuer, clinicians may provide advice, give in to specific demands, make decisions, and even assume blame for their patients' failure to work toward change. As a result, clinicians may feel angry, manipulated, and deceived. Not surprisingly, by assuming the rescuer role, clinicians not only inadvertently reinforce feelings of helplessness among these patients, but also become embroiled in a re-enactment of their earliest relationship pattern (Beck, Freeman, & Associates, 1990). Redirecting and refocusing the patient toward finding their own solutions is recommended.

In hysterical patients the erotic transference—or transference love, which is a mixture of tender, erotic, and sexual feelings toward the clinician—tends to develop over a gradual period of time along with feelings of shame and embarrassment. On the other hand, histrionic personality disordered individuals can develop an erotized transference, which, unlike transference love, is characterized by the expectation of sexual gratification with the clinician. Typical countertransferences with erotic and erotized transferences are aloofness, anxiety, and exploitation. Essentially, these transferences need to be analyzed and understood, and the countertransferences monitored rather than acted out. A detailed discussion of the resolution of these erotic/erotized transference–countertransferences can be found in Gabbard (1994).

☐ Pattern Analysis Strategies

Pattern analysis with histrionic personality disordered individuals involves an accurate diagnostic and clinical evaluation of schemas, styles, and triggering stressors, as well as level of functioning and readiness for therapeutic change. Knowledge of the optimal *DSM-IV* criterion along with the maladaptive pattern of the histrionic personality disordered individual is not only useful in specifying diagnosis but also in planning treatment that is tailored to the histrionic patient's unique style, needs, and circumstances. The optimal criterion specified for the histrionic personality disorder is discomfort in situations in which he or she is not the center of attention (Allnutt & Links, 1996). Both planned treatment goals and interventions should reflect this theme of attention-getting and specialness.

Pattern refers to the predictable and consistent style and manner in which a patient thinks, feels, acts, copes and defend the self. Pattern analysis involves both the triggers and response—the "what"—as well as an explanatory statement—the "why"—about the pattern of a given narcissistic patient. Obviously, such a clinical formulation specifies the *particular* schemas and temperamental styles unique to a given individual rather than the more *general* clinical formulation that will be noted here.

Triggers

Generally speaking, the "triggers" or "triggering" situations for histrionic patients are stressors related to heterosexual relationships (Othmer & Othmer, 1994). This means that when histrionic-disordered individuals are engaging in behaviors, discussing, or even thinking about certain opposite sex relationships and they become distressed, their disordered or maladaptive pattern is likely to be triggered, and their characteristic symptomatic affects, behaviors, and cognitions will be experienced or exhibited. Generally speaking, while histrionic patients tend to engage in help-seeking, seductive or attention-getting behavior with opposite sex individuals, they are more likely to engage in power struggles with same sex individuals.

Schemas

Generally speaking, the underlying schemas involve a self view of needing to be noticed by others, and a view of the world as the provider of special care and consideration because life makes them nervous (Sperry & Mosak, 1996). Among the most frequently encountered schema in histrionic patients is the entitlement/self-centeredness schema. Often, features of the emotional deprivation schema are also noted. The *entitlement/self-centeredness schema* refers to the core set of beliefs that one is entitled to take or receive whatever is wanted irrespective of the cost to others or society. The *emotional deprivation schema* refers to the core set of beliefs that one's need for nurturance and emotional support will never be met by others (Bricker, Young, & Flanagan, 1993; Young, 1994).

Style/Temperament

There are three style or temperament dimensions that may need to be addressed in formulating treatment with the histrionic personality: affective, behavioral–relational, and cognitive. Needless to say, these styles exacerbate and are exacerbated by their schemas. Histrionic individuals are prone to superficial, overmodulated affects. Behaviorally, they tend to be unfocused and inconsistent, whereas relationally they are likely to have difficulty relating to others except in superficial, manipulative manner. In addition, they tend to have empathic deficits. Finally, their cognitive style is marked by the capacity for global, impressionistic thinking, and vividness of imagination. They also experience considerable difficulty focusing on specifics and details. When impulsivity is also present, it further exacerbates the other style dysregulations. The most notable skill deficits in this disorder are problem-solving skills and self-management skills. Other skill deficits that may be present include empathy and time and money management.

☐ Pattern Change Strategies

In general, the overall goal of treatment with histrionic personality disordered individuals is to increase their capacity for reflection, interdependence, and self-management. In other words, the first goal is to "feel less and think more," which is the converse of the goal for the obsessive compulsive personality disorder. The goal of interdependence is met when the histrionic individual is able to establish and maintain more functional intimate relationships. That means that instead of relating to others in the demanding but distancing role of princess or sex object, the female histrionic can relate more as an intimate, equal partner taking the risks that mutually giving relationships require. Accomplishing these goals involves modifying maladaptive beliefs about specialness and attention-getting, and learning ways in which to increase self-management.

    After the maladaptive pattern has been identified and analyzed in terms of schemas, style and skill deficits, the therapeutic process involves relinquishing that pattern and replacing it with a more adaptive one. Thus, the pattern change process involves modifying schemas, modulating style dysregulations and reversing skill deficits. The process of modifying the maladaptive schemas of histrionic personality disordered patients usually follows efforts to modify style and skill-deficit dimensions because schema change early in the course of treatment is often resisted by the patient.

Schema Change

The entitlement/self-centered schema is supported by such injunctive beliefs as "I'm interesting and exciting," "Intuition and feeling are more important than rational planning," "If I'm entertaining others won't notice my weaknesses," and, particularly, "To be happy I need other people to pay attention to me" (Beck, Freeman, & Associates, 1990). The emotional deprivation schema fosters such histrionic beliefs as "I'll never get enough love and attention" and "I'm only capable of having superficial relationships" (Young, 1994). In the schema change process, the clinician and patient work collaboratively to understand the developmental roots of the maladaptive schemas. Then these schemas are tested through predictive experiments, guided observation, and reenactment of early schema-related incidents. Finally, histrionic patients are directed to begin to notice and remember counterschema data about themselves and their social experiences.

Style/Temperament Change

Because histrionic individuals tend to exhibit superficial but intense and overly modulated affects, emotional awareness training along with "dramatic behavioral experiments" can be effective interventions. Because of their flair for the dramatic and dread of protocol and detail, histrionic patients will likely respond to homework assignments if they are given permission to use their vivid imagination particularly with behavioral experiments and behavioral rehearsal. Beck, Freeman, and Associates (1990) illustrated the use of dramatic behavioral experiments with histrionic patients.

Problem solving training can be effective in assisting histrionic patients to become more organized and exert more consistent effort in daily life. Adding a measure of structure in their lives can reasonably modulate their free-spirited, inconsistent, and manipulative style. Because impulsivity is usually part of this style and can also exacerbate other style dysregulation, impulse control training may be necessary. Furthermore, because they tend to have some deficits in assertiveness, empathy and intimacy, assertive communication training, empathy training, and intimacy promoting activities may be indicated.

Setting specific treatment goals and learning the skill of listing advantages and disadvantages or pros and cons are common cognitive therapy interventions for modifying the personality's cognitive style (Beck, Freeman, & Associates, 1990). As noted below, medication may also be a useful adjunct in modulating these style dimensions.

Medication Strategies

Histrionic personality disordered individuals may exhibit Axis I diagnoses, including anxiety disorders, depressive disorders and somataform symptoms. When moderate to severe anxiety or depression is the presenting Axis I symptom, antidepressants may be indicated. When the presentation involves craving attention, exquisite rejection sensitivity, demanding behavior, and hypersomnia, the clinician should rule out the possibility that "hysteroid dysphoria" may be present; therefore, a monoamine oxidase inhibitor (MAOI) might be considered. When no obvious Axis I is present but affective instability and impulsivity are noted—often in lower functioning histrionic patients—sertraline, fluoxetine, or other selective serotonergic reuptake inhibitors have shown some benefit with such histrionic patients (Kavoussi, Liu, & Chaucer, 1994). However, often temperament or style dysregulations can only effectively be modulated with skill training.

Group Treatment Strategies

Group treatments have a number of advantages over individual treatment. First, group treatment frustrates the histrionic's wish and demand for the exclusive attention of the therapist. Group dynamics inevitably challenge the approval-seeking posture of these patients. Accordingly, the likelihood that an eroticized transference will develop is relatively small in contrast with individual therapy. Second, the histrionic patient's global cognitive style and related defenses of denial and repression can be more effectively modified in a group rather than an individual treatment context. These features are frustrating for group members who will subsequently confront the histrionic patient's distorted self-perceptions, omission of details, and thematic thinking. Third, because histrionic patients crave positive maternal transference, they expect, and even demand, that the group provide them with the maternal nurturance they missed as children. While the nurturing maternal transference can be particularly challenging in individual therapy, the group treatment context effectively diminishes this transference (Gabbard, 1994). These advantages are particularly relevant with lower to moderate functioning histrionic patients.

The following are some indications and contraindications for group treatment of the histrionic personality. Indications for group treatment include higher functioning histrionic individuals who can express affects directly and spontaneously, and those who can draw others out and manifest concern for other group members. Such individuals tend to be highly valued by other group members. Contraindications include histrionic patients who cannot participate in a group process without monopolizing or disrupting it. Nevertheless, clinical experience suggests that concurrent individual psychotherapy with group therapy can be useful for histrionic patients who are likely to monopolize or be disruptive in group settings. It should also be noted that skill-oriented groups are well-suited for lower functioning histrionic patients, particularly in partial hospitalization and day-treatment programs.

Marital and Family Therapy Strategies

Little has been written about family therapy, per se, with histrionic patients. However, there is considerable literature on couples therapy with histrionic patients. Typically, the marriage consists of a histrionic wife and an obsessive-compulsive husband, wherein the obsessive-compulsive partner has assumed increasing responsibility for the relationship while the histrionic partner has assumed an increasingly helpless or irresponsible role (Sperry & Maniacci, 1998). Treatment is often sought after a primitive outburst, which usually involves some actual or threatened self-destructive behavior, often in the context of a separation or divorce. The perceived or actual loss of a stable dependent person in their lives is a major stressor for histrionic patients. Thus, they will engage in various forms of attention-seeking behavior—including suicide gestures and promiscuity—in an effort to get the other partner's attention (Harbir, 1981). Generally, the goal of treatment is to change this pattern and redirect the energies of both partners. Usually, this goal can better be accomplished in conjoint rather than individual treatment. Sperry and Maniacci (1998) described an integrative dynamic, cognitive–behavioral and systems treatment approach for this type of couple.

Combined and Integrated Treatment Strategies

Integrated and combined treatment strategies are not only useful for higher functioning histrionic patients, they can considerably shorten the course of treatment. However, with lower to moderate functioning histrionic patients, integrated and combined treatment strategies are necessary for effective treatment outcomes. The most common combination of treatment modalities for moderate to higher functioning histrionic patients are individual therapy and couples or marital therapy, and individual therapy and heterogeneous group therapy. For lower functioning histrionic patients, skill-focused group treatment is particularly useful. Typically, this modality is combined with individual treatment. Previously, it was mentioned that concurrent individual psychotherapy is a necessary adjunct to group therapy for histrionic patients who monopolized the group process or were otherwise disruptive in group settings. Finally, medications may be a useful adjunct to psychotherapy, either concurrent or in tandem, if specific Axis I or Axis II target symptoms are prominent.

☐ Pattern Maintenance and Termination Strategies

Termination Issues

Treatment termination can be difficult and challenging for clinicians and histrionic patients, largely because the therapeutic relationship provided patients with undivided attention and concern. As the termination phase begins, a repetition of the maladaptive histrionic pattern is inevitable as they begin to realize that they must soon relinquish the attention and nurturance that treatment has come to represent. Fantasies of rescue and nurture that previously had remained veiled will now be disclosed. Particularly prominent are fantasies of a continued relationship with the clinician following termination. But since they have already relinquished much of their maladaptive pattern, these fantasies and yearnings are no longer as compelling as before. Presumably, they have also developed more adaptive relationships with significant others since treatment began. Accordingly, they can better tolerate the perceived loss of the therapeutic relationship. Subsequently, residual symptoms will finally be relinquished during this last phase of treatment, particularly those symptoms that were maintained become of secondary gain.

Allen (1977) noted that "the patient may have a covert wish for indefinite continuation of treatment, and only in the termination phase is it possible to examine and resolve the desperate need for an enduring, sustaining relationship" (p. 320). Furthermore, all the patient's dilemmas about relating to others, getting attention, and authentic sexuality can now be reviewed in the context of terminating the therapeutic relationship. Not surprisingly, as termination nears and their anxiety mounts, some patients attempt to continue a transference as a defense against the risk of establishing and maintaining real relationships outside the treatment context.

Two therapeutic strategies can facilitate the termination process. First, the clinician can offer the predictive interpretation that attention-getting and dependency needs may complicate the termination process. Conveying this prediction to the patient in a matter-of-fact, nonjudgmental fashion can simultaneously preempt the patient's conscious or unconscious wish to subvert termination and continue therapy indefinitely, and provide the patient with useful feedback regarding the ways in which their strivings can adversely affect other important interpersonal relationships. Second, spacing out sessions allows patients to become less reliant on their relationship with the clinician and more on relationships outside the treatment context. As they become increasing able to tolerate this separation, their maladaptive pattern shifts to a more adaptive and healthier pattern of interdependence.

Relapse Prevention Strategies

Another essential aspect of the treatment plan and process is relapse prevention. Because histrionic patients can easily revert to their maladaptive pattern, it is necessary to predict and plan for relapse. The final phase of treatment should largely focus on relapse prevention. An important goal of relapse prevention is predicting likely difficulties in the time period immediately following termination. Histrionic patients need to be able to analyze specific external situations such as persons, times, places, and internal states such as specific histrionic beliefs and fears, and other vulnerabilities that increase the likelihood of them responding with histrionic behavior in the face of predictable triggers. Once predicted, a contingency plan to deal with these stressors can be developed. Clinicians may find it useful to have patients think and talk through the following questions: What can I do if I find myself wanting to impress others or show off? What should I do if I start placing unreasonable demands on important relationships? What should I do if I start believing my old histrionic beliefs more than my new beliefs ? What should I do if I relapse? Finally, because interpersonal relationships are triggers for the histrionic pattern, the relapse plan should also include provisions for increasing and maintaining intimacy and commitment.

☐ Case Example

Kristy G. is a 44-year-old, married female who worked as a beauty consultant for a major cosmetics distributor. She had been married to Warren G. for 19 years and had an 18-year-old son. For the past 5 years she had been in psychiatric treatment for chronic, recurrent depression. Irrespective of the medications used, she experienced only partial remission of her symptoms and reported episodic periods of dysphoria, vague suicidal ideation, and chronic dissatisfaction with her life. She had also received adjunctive supportive psychotherapy from a social worker who claimed that "adjustment to her condition" was all she could expect from treatment. During her third year of treatment, Kristy realized that while she was not improving, her marriage was deteriorating. Her husband, who has been always been a pillar of strength for her, was becoming quite symptomatic himself and their relationship had become even more distant. Accordingly, she decided to stop her current treatment and try couples therapy. Subsequently, she and her husband met with a couples therapist who, after evaluating them as a couple in a conjoint session and then also individually, recommended a course of conjoint couples and also dynamically oriented individual psychotherapy for both spouses. The course of couples therapy is described in some detail in conjunction with the case of Warren G. in Chapter 9 of this book, while the course of individual treatment with Kristy is described here.

Engagement Process

Kristy was an attractive woman who was quite fashionably dressed yet appeared somewhat older than her stated age. She appeared to be considerably pleased with the prospect of working with a male clinician. Despite her somewhat depressed mood, she forced smiles, gesticulated with her hands, made facial expressions that seemed exaggerated, and gave the impression she was performing for an admiring but unseen audience. Initially skeptical of combining dynamically oriented individual therapy with couples sessions, Kristy agreed to the treatment plan.

Pattern Analysis

Kristy was the youngest of four siblings and a prized daughter, particularly of her father. She was especially cute and received considerable attention for her brightness and vivaciousness. Shortly after her third birthday, her mother was admitted for the first of several hospitalizations for depression. This illness took its toll on the rest of the family. The father was forced to take on an additional job and withdrew much of his attention from Kristy. While she was still the favorite grandchild of her grandparents, she secretly envied mother's new, privileged position. Mother gained

considerable sympathy and seemed to be excused from much of the bur-
den of being housewife and mother. Her needs always seemed to prevail,
and, not surprisingly, the family byword was "Don't upset your mother!"
Kristy's first episode of depression occurred when she 15 years old following the breakup of an intense relationship with her 18-year-old boyfriend
who had left to attend the university. She felt devastated and claims to
have never fully gotten over this loss. She eventually completed training
as a cosmetologist and after which she has been successfully employed as
a beauty consultant.

Her earliest memory involved her fourth birthday party. She was
wearing a party dress and everyone was looking admiringly at her. She
felt special, loved, and amazed by all the gifts and the cake that were placed
before her. Her next memory involved her first day of school. She recalls
walking into class, feeling pretty in a new dress. The female teacher told
her she needed to take a seat near the back of the room since her name
was near the end of the alphabet. Her first reaction was to look at the
teacher, but then at herself, thinking she wasn't dressed "nice enough" to
be up front. She felt angry and sad. These early recollections, along with
other developmental history data, suggested that Kristy had internalized
the schemas of entitlement/self-centeredness and emotional deprivation
indicative of the histrionic personality. Her overmodulated affects, impressionistic thinking and deficits in intimacy, empathy and other interpersonal skills were also indicative of the histrionic personality. She met criteria for dysthymic disorder as well as histrionic personality disorder with
narcissistic features. Her current level of functioning was fair (GAF score
of 55) although she had functioned better earlier in the year (GAF score of
67). Her current level of distress she was experiencing in herself and in her
family, along with her husband's willingness to seek couples therapy with
her, suggested that her motivation and readiness was reasonably high and
predictive of a positive treatment outcome.

The following pattern formulation served as basis for planning individual treatment. Kristy grew up feeling special but cheated. Although she
was aware that she could get attention for her specialness, she was also
aware of how fleeting it could be. Getting attention was wonderful, but
being able to hold on to it was another matter. She measured life and
others by how they could care for her and notice her. Not surprisingly, she
mastered the art of attracting others' attention. As she grew older, she
thought her specialness, particularly her beauty, youth, and energy were
beginning to fade. She felt abandoned by her husband who worked long
hours, and anticipated she would also be abandoned by her son who would
soon be leaving for college, as her first love had. She was using depression
as a coping device to deal with life, to draw others to her as she had seen
modeled by her mother. She was probably genetically loaded for depres-

sion and had become skilled, like her mother, in using it to rally support for herself. Figure 8.1 summarizes these style features.

Pattern Change

Since she had experienced only partial symptomatic relief from several antidepressant trials over the previous 5 years, Kristy's depressive symptoms were framed as persistent symptoms that were more likely to respond to psychosocial interventions like symptom management training

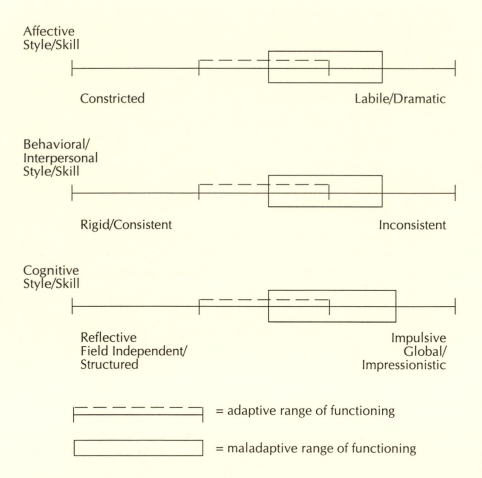

FIGURE 8.1. Style/skill dimensions of histrionic personality disorder.

and cognitive therapy. Accordingly, individual treatment sessions initially focused on learning the symptom management skill of distraction, which she agreed to practice between sessions. Concurrently, treatment also focused on her dysthymic features using the short-term cognitive therapy treatment protocol for dysthymia described by Freeman (1992). Kristy was helped to identify her negative thoughts and cognitive distortion and challenge them. The 26 individual sessions, supported by her couples therapy, allowed Kristy to gain considerable control over her chronic depression and dissatisfaction. Her scattered, inconsistent behavior style, which was reinforced by her impressionistic cognitive style, was modulated to some degree with problem solving training and assertive communication training. In the course of these in-session and between-session activities, she learned to take more control of her life by being better organized and more decisive. Empathy training and work on intimacy skills was accomplished in conjoint sessions with her husband (cf. the case example in Chapter 9).

Finally, schema change strategies were used to modify her entitlement/self-centeredness and emotional deprivation schemas.

Pattern Maintenance and Termination

During the termination phase, Kristy's dysthymia became more under her control and she experienced more satisfaction in life and with her marriage. Her relationship with her husband was greatly improved, in part because of the couples therapy, and part because he was now working out of a home office which meant he and Kristy were able to spend more time together. She also reported less fear about her future, her marriage, and her son. She began to feel more consistency and balance in her life. While she still enjoyed dressing fashionably and remained free-spirited, she experienced herself as more connected and valued as a person. A planned termination from individual treatment occurred after 26 sessions. These sessions had been spaced over a period of 18 months. Four months prior to termination, couples therapy had been terminated. It was mutually agreed that quarterly follow-up sessions would be scheduled over the next year.

☐ Summary

Effective treatment of histrionic personality disorder requires that these patients become sufficiently committed to a treatment process that is tailored and focused on modifying their maladaptive histrionic pattern. Because these patients tend to have considerable difficulty engaging in and profiting from traditional psychotherapy, an integrative-combined approach that focuses on characterological, temperament, and skill dimensions is usually essential for effective treatment outcomes. The case example illustrates the common challenges that these patients present, and the kind of clinician flexibility and competence as well as treatment resources required. Table 8.2 summarizes the treatment intervention strategies most likely to be effective with this disorder.

TABLE 8.2.   Treatment Interventions with Histrionic Personality Disorder

Phase	Issue	Strategy/Tactic
Engagement	Quickly develops therapeutic alliance; Believes clinician should be able to understand them intuitively, nonverbally, without intrapsychic exploration	Role induction and socialization; Reflection vs. impressionistic reporting
Transference	Rescue fantasy; Erotic or eroticized transference	Redirect and refocus; Analyse and explain
Countertransference	Messiah/rescue role; Aloofness, anxiety; Exploitation	Monitor and refrain from acting out
Pattern Search	**Triggers:** opposite sex relationships	
Pattern Change	**Treatment Goals:** feel less, think more; Increased interdependence and self-management	

Table 8.2 continued on page 165.

TABLE 8.2. *Continued*

Phase	Issue	Strategy/Tactic
Schema/Character	Entitlement/self-centeredness schema; Emotional deprivation schema	Schema change strategy; Interpretation strategy
Style/Temperament		
a. Affective Style	Superficial, over-modulated effects	Emotional awareness training; Dramatic behavioral experiments; Externalization of voices
b. Behavioral/ Relational Style	Inconsistency; Over/underassertive; Empathy and intimacy deficits	Problem solving training; Intimacy skills; Empathy training
c. Cognitive Style	Global/impressionistic Impulsivity	Set specific treatment goals; Pros and cons analysis; Impulse control training
Maintenance/ Termination	Fantasies of a continuing relationship; Fear of termination	Predictive interpretation; Weaning, spaced sessions; Encourage other healthy relationships

Obsessive-Compulsive Personality Disorder

The obsessive-compulsive personality disorder is characterized by rigidity, stubbornness, and judgmentalness; all factors that can impede personal change. Nevertheless, these individuals can be effectively treated, although the treatment of obsessive-compulsive personalities involves some unique therapeutic challenges. This chapter describes specific engagement, pattern analysis, pattern change, and pattern maintenance and termination strategies for effectively managing and treating this disorder. In addition to individual psychotherapeutic strategies and tactics, group, marital and family, medication, and integrative and combined treatment strategies are detailed. An extensive case example illustrates the treatment process. Before turning to treatment strategies, the DSM-IV description and criteria are briefly presented.

☐ DSM-IV Description and Criteria

DSM-IV offers the following description and criteria for obsessive-compulsive personality disorder:

TABLE 9.1: DSM-IV Description and Criteria for Obsessive-
Compulsive Personality Disorder

301.4 Obsessive-Compulsive Personality Disorder

"A pervasive pattern of preoccupation with orderliness, perfectionism, and mental and interpersonal control, at the expense of flexibility, openness, and efficiency, beginning by early adulthood and present in a variety of contexts, as indicated by four (or more) of the following:

(1) is preoccupied with details, rules, lists, order, organization, or schedules to the extent that the major point of the activity is lost

(2) shows perfectionism that interferes with task completion (e.g., is unable to complete a project because his or her own overly strict standards are not met)

(3) is excessively devoted to work and productivity to the exclusion of leisure activities and friendships (not accounted for by obvious economic necessity)

(4) is overconscientious, scrupulous, and inflexible about matters or morality, ethics, or values (not accounted for by cultural or religious identification)

(5) is unable to discard worn-out or worthless objects even when they have no sentimental value

(6) is reluctant to delegate tasks or to work with others unless they submit to exactly his or her way of doing things

(7) adopts a miserly spending style toward both self and others; money is viewed as something to be hoarded for future catastrophes

(8) shows rigidity and stubbornness"

☐ Engagement Strategies

Early Session Behavior

The characteristic features of circumstantiality, perfectionism, and ambivalence make interviewing obsessive-compulsive individuals difficult and challenging. Their preoccupation with details and their need for control often results in a seemingly endless struggle about facts, issues, and power struggles. Clinicians who persist in asking open-ended questions will note that while they become frustrated, obsessive-compulsive individuals become confused. These patients are better able to handle more focused questions, although they have a tendency to interpret them too narrowly. They may bring copies of past treatment records or a notebook that details their medical history, diet, and exercise pattern, and possibly their dreams. Usually, they expect the clinician to review these documents or topics in detail. Because these details are important to the obsessive-compulsive's self-definition, it is important that the clinician acknowledges this offer rather than preemptorily dismissing it. Expressing affects are difficult because these individuals believe emotional expression is dangerous or at least suspect. Although they may admit that affects are associated with details, they will discount the value of expressing those affects, much less talking about them. Furthermore, it is difficult for them to overcome their ambivalence because they will not easily accept the clinician's assurance that their problems are solvable or that relinquishing control of their life is tolerate.

Because they insist they are objective and have no feelings, they are perturbed at the clinician's expression of empathy and reject it as irrelevant. The clinician's only effective therapeutic leverage with these patients is to get and keep them in touch with their anger and other affects. Initially, they will defend against or deny these affects, and use additional obsessionality to neutralize such therapeutic leverage. In sum, forming a therapeutic alliance is difficult and early sessions may consists of aborted attempts, frustrations and struggles (Othmer & Othmer, 1994).

Facilitating Collaboration

True collaboration is extremely difficult to achieve early in the course of treatment of the obsessive-compulsive personality disorder. Rather, pseudo-collaboration tends to occur quickly. *Pseudo-collaboration* refers to behaviors that, at first, may appear to be collaborative and cooperative behaviors but are not. These patients may appear to be eager to be "model" patients and attempt to please the clinician by being "prepared" for sessions. For example, they may come to sessions with lists of items that they are prepared to discuss, diaries that detail dreams, and the like, or they may have overachieved on a between-session or homework assignment. However, the veneer of their "collaboration" is quickly revealed when the clinician endeavors to ask about their feelings and fears, or attempts to focus on the present rather than the past. Typically, they will resist requests to share affects and are uncomfortable commenting on the "here and now" of the clinician–patient relationship. Such responses are reflective of their ambivalence, the need to please vs. the need to control, as well as their belief that life is unpredictable and so must take control or, at least, resist efforts to be controlled. For the obsessive-compulsive individual, rational expression is much more predictable and comfortable than expression of affects, which are much less predictable and comfortable. Whereas facts can bolster their perceived sense of self-worth, feelings threaten to embarrass or even injure them. Similarly, the patient will "structure" sessions with their planned agenda to reduce the unpredictable.

True collaboration will occur only when the obsessive-compulsive patient experiences minimal threat in treatment. Accordingly, the clinician is advised to establish a "collaborative contract," which is based on the patient's goal for treatment. The goal, a method for achieving the goal, and specific role expectations for both clinician and patient are stated. For example, the patient's goal might be "to increase my efficiency," while problem solving is indicated as the primary treatment strategy or method to achieve the goal. A problem-solving treatment strategy is an excellent way of operationalizing the collaborative contract. It consists of stating a goal or analyzing a problem, identifying options, weighing the options, deciding on a course of action, and then implementing it. Besides being effective, this treatment strategy is usually quite acceptable to the obsessive patient since it is rational and is relatively nonthreatening. In addition, the clinician needs to structure sessions in such a way that threat is minimized and treatment goals can be achieved. This means focusing on one topic at a time and confronting resistances as they arise. Not surprisingly, the cognitive-behavioral approach is well suited for working with obsessive-compulsive patients.

Transference and Countertransference

Predictable transference and countertransference problems are noted in treating obsessive-compulsive personality disordered individuals. Perhaps the most common transference involve their tendency to engage in rambling speech, often in a monotone. The defenses of intellectualization and isolation of affect are commonly noted. In the process, they wander from their original point and create an "anesthetizing cloud," which serves both as a smoke screen to mask their feeling and to sidetrack the clinician's attention (Gabbard, 1994). Not surprisingly, the related countertransference to this rambling is boredom, daydreaming, and disengagement. Sometimes, these monologues may have high interest for the clinician, and the clinician may be tempted to reinforce or collude with the patient's intellectualization and isolation of affect. The clinician does well to interrupt, interpret, or redirect these rambling accounts. Saying "Let's just stop for a moment. What are you feeling right now?" can refocus and set the stage for interpreting resistance.

For some obsessive-compulsive patients, clinical and transference interpretations can be quite threatening and are consequently vigorously resisted. A related transference involves patient discounting of the clinician's interpretations. The patient may quickly respond to an interpretation saying it is completely wrong or that he's thought about or heard it before and didn't agree with it then or now. The clinician's countertransference may range from self-doubt and cautiousness to anger and hostility at the patient's impertinence and unappreciativeness.

☐ Pattern Analysis Strategies

Pattern analysis with obsessive-compulsive individuals involves an accurate diagnostic and clinical evaluation of schemas, styles, and triggering stressors, as well as level of functioning and readiness for therapeutic change. Knowledge of the optimal DSM-IV criterion along with the maladaptive pattern of the individual is not only useful in specifying diagnosis but also in planning treatment that is tailored to the obsessive-compulsive patient's unique style, needs, and circumstances. The optimal criterion specified for the obsessive-compulsive personality disorder is showing perfectionism that interferes with task completion (Allnutt & Links, 1996). Both planned treatment goals and interventions should reflect this theme of perfectionism.

Pattern refers to the predictable and consistent style and manner in which a patient thinks, feels, acts, copes and defends the self. Pattern analysis involves both the triggers and response—the "what"—as well as an explanatory statement—the "why"—about the pattern of a given narcissistic patient. Obviously, such a clinical formulation specifies the *particular* schemas and temperamental styles unique to a given individual rather than the more *general* clinical formulation that will be noted here.

Triggers

Generally speaking, the "triggers" or "triggering" situations for obsessive-compulsive patients are stressors related to authority, unstructured situations, or close relationships (Othmer & Othmer, 1994). This means that when obsessive-compulsive-disordered individuals are engaging in behaviors, discussing, or even thinking about the demands of authority figures or close relationships or being in situations where expectations for them are unclear and they become distressed, their disordered or maladaptive pattern is likely to be triggered and characteristic symptomatic effects, behaviors, and cognitions are likely to be experienced or exhibited.

Schemas

Generally speaking, the underlying schemas involve a self-view of being responsible for not making errors, and a view of the world as overly demanding and unpredictable (Sperry & Mosak, 1996). Among the most frequently encountered schemas in obsessive-compulsive patients is the unrelenting/unbalanced schema. Occasionally, the emotional inhibition schema is also observed. The *unrelenting/unbalanced schema* refers to the core set of beliefs about the relentless striving to meet high flown expectations of oneself at the expense of happiness, health and satisfying relationships. The *emotional inhibition schema* refers to the core set of beliefs that emotions and impulses must be inhibited in order not to lose self-esteem or harm others (Bricker, Young, & Flanagan, 1993; Young, 1994).

Style/Temperament

There are three style/temperaments that may need to be addressed in formulating treatment with the obsessive-compulsive personality: affective, behavioral–interpersonal, and cognitive. Needless to say, these styles exacerbate and are exacerbated by their schemas. The affective style of obsessive-compulsive individuals is characterized by constriction and isolation of affect. Their cognitive style is ruminative and overly reflective, which predisposes them to preoccupation with details and minutia as well as worry. Behaviorally, their style is rigid and calculating, which, together with their ruminative style, predisposes them to procrastination and indecisiveness. Relationally, they are inhibited and ill at ease. Not surprisingly, they tend to be deficient in empathy and other interpersonal skills.

☐ Pattern Change Strategies

At the outset of treatment, it would not be unusual for obsessive-compulsive individuals to have as their personal goal of treatment to become asymptomatic and more productive while retaining their maladaptive pattern. This contrasts with the therapeutic treatment goal, which is to change the maladaptive pattern. More specifically, the general treatment goal for obsessive-compulsive individuals is to achieve balance between perfectionism and driveness and being easy going and carefree, to become introspective without preoccupation and rumination, and to better tolerate the humanness they observe in themselves and others. In other words, the goal is to "think less and feel more," which is the converse of the goal for the histrionic personality disorder.

Treatment begins after the maladaptive pattern has been identified and analyzed in terms of schemas, style, and skill deficits. The therapeutic process involves relinquishing that pattern and replacing it with a more adaptive pattern. This pattern change process involves modifying schemas, modulating style dysregulations, and reversing skill deficits. The process of modifying the maladaptive schemas usually follows efforts to modify style and skill-deficit dimensions because schema change early in the course of treatment is often resisted by the patient. It is for this reason that, as noted in the section on facilitating collaboration, treatment should begin by using a problem-solving treatment strategy. This strategy is not only effective in establishing a collaborative relationship, but also for making initial changes in pattern. This strategy is greatly appreciated by obsessive patients because it is rational and systematic and is much less threatening and anxiety-producing than dynamic or experiential intervention strategies.

Schema Change

The unrelenting/unbalanced standards and emotional inhibition schemas are supported by such injunctive beliefs as "Nothing I do is really good enough, I must always do better;" "I need to be in total control of my feelings;" "Details are extremely important;" "If I don't perform at the highest possible level, I'm a failure;" and "Mistakes, errors and defects are absolutely intolerable" (Beck, Freeman, & Associates, 1990; Young, 1994).

In the schema change process, the clinician and patient work collaboratively to understand the developmental roots of the maladaptive schemas. Then, these schemas are tested through predictive experiments, guided observation, and reenactment of early schema-related incidents. Finally, obsessive-compulsive patients are directed to begin to notice and remember counterschema data about themselves and their social experiences.

Style/Temperament Change

Because obsessive-compulsive individuals are characterized by an affective style of constriction and isolation of affect, emotional awareness training can be an effective intervention. Thought stopping training can be useful in reducing ruminative thinking. Furthermore, because these patients tend to have behavioral and relational styles that are somewhat inhibited and stiff, and often have deficits in empathy and other interpersonal skills training and empathy training may be indicated. Furthermore, activity scheduling (Freeman, Pretzer, Fleming, & Simon, 1990) can be effectively used in reducing procrastination and better managing time.

Medication Strategies

Concurrent Axis I conditions, particularly anxiety and depressive disorders, may be amenable to medication. Interestingly, although cyclic antidepressants, serotonergic blockers, monoamine oxidase inhibitors, lithium carbonate, antipsychotics, and anxiolytic have been effective with obsessive-compulsive disorder, these same medications have little or no effect on obsessive-compulsive personality disorder (Jenike, 1991). Accordingly, psychotherapy is the treatment of choice for this disorder.

Group Treatment Strategies

A major deficit of this disorder is the inability to share tenderly and spontaneously with others. Thus, group treatment can be particularly useful with obsessive-compulsive patients. Nevertheless, because these patients tend to be competitive and controlling, certain complications can arise which the clinicians would do well to keep in mind. For instance, these patients will dominate a group with their rambling and excessive speech patterns if not redirected. Because they may initially experience the affective atmosphere in a group to be overwhelming, they may become more socially isolated or intellectually detached. Thus, the clinician does well to intervene to avoid unnecessary power struggles. When this is accomplished, these patients are usually able to vicariously model the emotional expressiveness of others in the group.

Group therapy offers a number of advantages over individual therapy for the obsessive-compulsive patients. First, this personality pattern tends to make the individual therapy process tedious, difficult, and unrewarding, particularly early in treatment when clinicians commonly err with premature interpretations or behavioral prescriptions. Second, the group process tends to diffuse the intensity of the obsessive-compulsive patient's impact, particularly in a heterogenous group. Third, group treatment also tends to neutralize transferences and countertransferences because patients more easily accept feedback from peers than from a clinician. Finally, group therapy activates these patients into "experiencing" their problems rather than just talking about them.

There are, however, some contraindications for outpatient group therapy for obsessive-compulsive patients: severe depression or high suicidality; impulsive dyscontrol; strong paranoid propensities; acute crisis; difficulty in establishing trust; fear of relinquishing obsessive-compulsive defenses; the need to establish superiority; and the use of "pseudo insight" to avoid dealing with both hostile and tender feelings (Wells, Glickhauf-Hughes, & Buzzel, 1990). Nevertheless, such patients or other lower functioning obsessive-compulsive patients may still be candidates for skill-oriented group treatment in partial hospital or day programs.

Wells et al. (1990) described a group treatment approach that is well-suited for obsessive-compulsive patients. This approach combines both interpersonal and psychodynamic interventions. The treatment process involves the following goals: modifying cognitive style, resolving control issues, expanding decision-making and action-taking capacity, modifying harsh superego, increasing comfort with emotional expression, and modifying interpersonal style.

Marital and Family Therapy Strategies

Harbir (1981) reported that obsessive-compulsive individuals usually agree to family treatment because close family members have become angry with their rigidity, procrastination, constricted affect, perfectionism, and pessimistic outlook. Likewise, the obsessive-compulsive individual may agree to couples therapy only after being threatened with divorce by their partner. Often, a threat of separation or divorce may be the only motivation to start treatment. The anxiety of the complaining partner may be the only leverage for treatment, and the clinician may need to work with that partner to deal more effectively with the other partner's obsessive-compulsive personality pattern. Clinical experience suggests that obsessive-compulsive individuals tend to marry histrionic individuals (Sperry & Maniacci, 1998).

Salzman (1989) noted that obsessive-compulsive patients who are highly anxious may be unable to participate in marital or family therapy until their anxiety has been sufficiently quelled in individual psychotherapy or combined psychotherapy and pharmacological treatment. Even when excessive anxiety is not particularly bothersome, these patients can be tyrants in family sessions, and may immobilize other family members to such an extent that treatment is jeopardized. When this occurs, structural and strategic intervention directed at redistributing power may be particularly advantageous in such situations (Sperry, 1995).

Combined and Integrated Treatment Strategies

Salzman (1989) contended that a combined/integrated approach is essential in the treatment of the obsessive-compulsive disorder, particularly for moderately severe cases. He insisted that the various treatment modalities and methods must be viewed as mutually inclusive rather than mutually exclusive.

Combined treatments tend to be more effective when based on a protocol. Because high levels of anxiety or depression will limit participation in psychotherapy, an appropriate trial of medication may be necessary at the onset of treatment. When rituals or obsessions are prominent, specific behavior interventions are probably indicated. The dynamics of perfectionism, indecisiveness, and isolation of affect are best addressed with specific psychotherapeutic interventions. Decisions about the use of individual, group, or a marital and module format, or a combination of modalities should be based on severity of the disorder, particular treatment targets, and specific contraindications to treatments.

In short, a fuller understanding and appreciation of the obsessive-compulsive personality usually requires an integration of several modalities because "the resolution of the disabling disorder demands cognitive clarity plus behavioral and physiologic alterations. Each modality alone deals with only a piece of the puzzle. A therapist who can combine all these approaches will be the most effective" (Salzman, 1989, p. 2782).

☐ Pattern Maintenance and Termination Strategies

Termination Issues

Just as establishing a collaborative relationship with obsessive-compulsive patients can be extremely difficult, so also is terminating treatment. Assuming they have achieved some level of balance between being perfectionistic and driven and being easy going and carefree, terminating treatment can be considered. Unfortunately, ambivalence, which is a core feature of the obsessive-compulsive pattern, is commonly observed during the termination process. Initially, these patients may press to leave treatment and function on their own. Soon thereafter, they begin expressing great reluctance to relinquish the security of therapy for the exigencies of the real world until there is absolute certainty that insurmountable problems will not occur. Consequently, they will insist on remaining in treatment. Salzman (1980) contended that these patients cannot be relied on to initiate discussion or press for termination. The clinician task is to raise the issue of readiness for termination, and then coax and prod them into the real world. Nevertheless, termination must be a gradual and empirical process. Unlike the fixed planned termination date that might be established with the dependent personality disordered patient, some measure of flexibility is more therapeutic with the obsessive-compulsive patients. After all, clinicians' insistence on setting strict deadlines and appointment scheduling is really an enactment of the rigidity and perfectionism that they are trying to modify in these patients.

Reducing the length of a session or spacing out sessions over a reasonable period of time allows these patients to more safely reenter the real world. This reduction can begin when patients become comfortable enough to accept some uncertainty and reverses in their lives without experiencing intolerable symptoms. For many obsessive-compulsive patients, the termination process can be expected to engender anxiety and/or somatic symptoms. They must come to understand and accept that such symptoms will occasionally occur throughout life and that treatment does not guarantee symptom-free living.

Relapse Prevention Strategies

After treatment is formally terminated, the option for occasional appointments or even brief contacts during times of crisis should be discussed. Some obsessive-compulsive patients will appreciate the offer of one or more planned follow-up visits in the subsequent 12 months. The hope, however, is that these patients will be able to function as their own clinicians. To this end, it is helpful for clinicians and patients to collaboratively develop a plan of self-therapy and relapse prevention following termination. It is recommended that these patients set aside an hour a week to engage in activities that continue the progress made in formal treatment. They might work on selected exercises. They might look ahead at the coming week and predict which situations could be troublesome. The goal of such effort is to maintain treatment gains, particularly their newly acquired pattern. They should expect to cope much more effectively than prior to treatment because they have developed sufficient personal and relational skills to be introspective, without preoccupation and rumination, and to tolerate more of the humanness they observe in themselves and others. And when they find themselves slipping or regressing they will know how to refocus and redirect themselves.

The relapse plan will help them analyze specific external situations (such as persons, times, places) and internal states (such as specific obsessive-compulsive beliefs and fears) and other vulnerabilities that increase the likelihood of them responding with histrionic behavior in the face of predictable triggers. Once predicted, a contingency plan to deal with these stressors can be developed. Clinicians may find it useful to have patients answer these questions: What can I do if I find myself ruminating? What should I do if I start placing unreasonable demands or expectations on others to be more perfect? What should I do if I start believing my old obsessive-compulsive beliefs more than my new beliefs? What should I do if I relapse? Finally, because relational demands, unstructured situations, and authority issues can trigger the obsessive-compulsive pattern, the relapse plan should also include provisions for increasing and maintaining playfulness and spontaneity.

☐ Case Example

Warren G. is a 41-year-old, married accountant who presented with his wife, Kristy G., for couples therapy. They have been married for 19 years and had an 18-year-old son who would soon be finishing high school and move away to attend college. He complained of worsening insomnia and decreased energy. In addition, his acrophobia had also worsened. He now had become so anxious crossing bridges and taking escalators, especially glass elevators, that he had to drive out of his way to get to his office building, and when there he would walk up seven flights of stairs to reach his office. He had been prescribed Ativan by his family physician but rarely used them fearing he would become addicted.

Warren reported significant strains in the marriage. He was concerned with his wife's safety, noting that she seemed more depressed and hopeless. He described Kristy as increasingly moody, unpredictable, and given to outbursts, which frustrated and frightened him. She would pursue him relentlessly with demands and all he could do was clam up and retreat. He hesitatingly admitted that it was a relief to stay late at his office so as not to face her fury. Lately, he feared he might lose his mind if this continued. His only display of emotion in the entire interview occurred then: He was briefly silent as tears welled in his eyes, but then he quickly regained composure.

Engagement Process—Warren

As part of the evaluation phase of couples therapy, he was scheduled for an individual evaluation session. During this session he seemed more at ease discussing concerns about the marriage than he was in the conjoint session. Nevertheless, he was somewhat reluctant in disclosing personal information. He was a methodical historian of the various details of his life. He spoke in a slow, deliberate monotone with little change in affect or mood. In addition to couples therapy, individual therapy was suggested to help Warren understand the marriage relationship and the effect it was having on him. Initially, he balked at individual sessions stating that he was more concerned with his wife's well-being, and that she was his first priority. Recognizing that Warren was likely resisting individual treatment believing that he must be dutiful and unselfish, the clinical made the following observations. He noted that while it was commendable to put his wife's concerns first, Warren also had worsening symptoms that were greatly worrisome to his wife. He gently reminded Warren that during their conjoint session Kristy had hoped that he would be receptive to individual sessions. Furthermore, the clinician emphasized that focusing on these matters from two perspectives, individual work and couples work, would be the most "efficient" approach. Warren liked that concept and agreed to the plan.

Engagement Process—Couple

It seemed clear that both partners wanted and needed help. However, because Kristy had been in long-term psychiatric treatment and so was perceived as a "patient," the clinician thought it necessary and useful to socialize Kristy and Warren to a systems perspective for the conjoint treatment. It was framed that neither of them were "sick" and that each was simply expressing in his or her characteristic style what neither had "permission" or "ability" to say with his or her mouth. Both responded favorably to this perspective. Warren was fascinated by the prospect that anything could occur beyond one's control. He knew it happened, he had seen it at work many times, but he never thought any such process would be going on in him without his knowing. Kristy was amused by his comment and pointed out that if he "knew" he was doing such things, he wouldn't be able to do them. She beamed at the clinician, as if waiting for a reward or praise. It was also framed that neither was "crazy" but, rather, both were attempting to communicate with the other. Not only did the receiving partner not understand the communication, the sending partner was not completely aware of the message. Thus, the first task of treatment was to accept responsibility for sending the message, that is, acknowledge that a message was being sent, and to then clarify the message. Only then, could each decide how to respond favorably to the message being sent.

Pattern Analysis—Warren

Warren described his childhood as "reasonably good," but went on to describe his father as a violent alcoholic with unpredictable mood swings, and his mother as a long suffering woman who leaned on Warren as her sole support. Warren had a younger sister who had cerebral palsy, and he recalled his father's frequent threats to institutionalize her. He took it on as his mission to keep her out of an institution and so became her surrogate parent, teacher, and friend. He worked outside the home from the age of 15. His first job had been on a loading dock amid much squalor. These experiences led him to vow to make a better life for himself, and never lose his temper nor to drink like his father. He eventually completed a GED, went to college, studied for and passed his CPA exam, and found employment with a small accounting firm. Although he agreed that he worked too many hours, he liked his job. Although there was little room for upward mobility there, he was proud that his boss entrusted him with complicated and sensitive projects that no one else could do as well as he.

His earliest memory occurred when he was on the fire escape of the family apartment at the age of five. As he was admiring the view he heard a scream. His mother rushed out and pulled him back into the apartment, yelling that it was too dangerous to be out on the fire escape. He felt confused but vowed to be more careful and never to upset her again.

Needless to say, Warren grew up believing that he had to be careful and conscientious or bad things would happen. Gradually, the line between conscientiousness and control began to blur, and unless he controlled his, and others, life, he sensed an uneasy, impending doom. His solution was to work harder, to control more, and to be careful. The only dispensation he allowed himself from this rigid agenda was illness. By being afraid of heights and unable to sleep, he could ask for a break and take some time for himself without having to admit that he was shirking responsibility.

An evaluation of Warren's developmental history and clinical observation of his interactions with Kristy indicated an obsessive-compulsive pattern. His pattern was notable for both the unrelenting/unbalanced and the emotional inhibition schemas. Style dimensions such as constricted affect, rigidity, empathic and interpersonal deficits, and analytic, ruminative cognitive style also suggested an obsessive-compulsive pattern. Warren met criteria for minor depressive disorder as well as obsessive-compulsive personality disorder. His current level of functioning was fair to good (GAD score of 61) and his best functioning in the past year had been good to very good (GAD score of 73). Because of his own willingness and efforts to make personal and relational changes, his motivation and readiness for treatment was rated as high. Figure 9.1 summarizes these style features.

Pattern Analysis—Couple

The interlocking dynamics gradually became clear to them. Kristy's depression was reframed as a way of asking to be cared for, and her "moodiness" as her trying to keep the relationship together. She valued love and the marriage and family, and she wanted them to be happy. She was trying to keep them together, and to look out for her husband and his health. Warren was trying to keep his family together too, and his long work hours were reframed as his way of showing caring and concern. In effect, they were told that their symptoms were serving the same purpose, just in different ways. The challenge for both of them was to communicate their desires in more direct, constructive ways.

Pattern Change—Couple

Pattern change involved rebalancing their relationship pattern. This proved exceedingly challenging, because power was rather evenly distributed: Warren was aloof, didactic, and in charge, until Kristy became upset and "hysterical," at which point she would regain power of the relationship. Then, Warren would calm the situation by arranging things the way she wanted. In the process, he would organize and structure the necessary changes and, thus, assume power again. She would allow this until she felt he cared more about his work than her, after which and she would grow impatient, become upset, and the cyclic pattern would repeat itself.

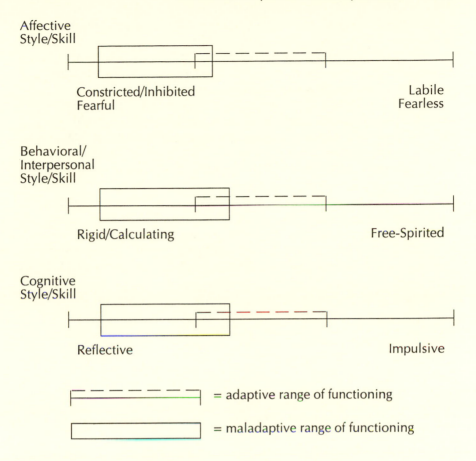

FIGURE 9.1. Style/skill dimensions of obsessive compulsive personality disorder.

This cyclic pattern was pointed out to them. Warren immediately grasped it and its ramifications, but Kristy found it harder to comprehend. The clinician's verbal explanation was well-suited to Warren's analytic style, but did not match Kristy's more global-impressionistic style. Furthermore, their maladaptive cyclic pattern was being enacted in the session. Warren shifted into his parental mode and began lecturing her, whereas Kristy shifted into her child mode and tried but couldn't follow his explanation. At that point the clinician graphically illustrated their interaction pattern and Kristy was then able to readily grasp it.

Boundaries and intimacy were not as easily addressed. A triangle existed, with their son vacillating between being a husband-surrogate for his mother when Warren was away from home, to his acting like a friend to his father when Warren was home. His presence both fueled the maladaptive cyclic pattern and perpetuated the very problems that, without his presence, might lead to some kind of resolution. The next several weeks of conjoint treatment focused on these issues. While there might be value in switching to a family therapy mode, there were inherent dangers as well. Introducing the son into conjoint sessions would perpetuate the very issue he was helping to maintain: intruding on the couple's relationship. Instead, efforts were undertaken to strengthen the couple's bond without the son in the session. Interpersonal skills training was begun. One component of the training was for the couple to go out on a date after each session. Relating intimately had been problematic for Warren because of deficits in empathic responding. Accordingly, three conjoint sessions focused on empathy training. In addition, the clinician framed to Warren that his son needed to "have space to find himself," while Warren needed to expand his own social network. To Kristy, it was framed that by encouraging her son to "separate," she would be strengthening both her marriage as well as her son's future. Both agreed to a "weaning" process that was aided by the son's move out of the city to attend college.

Warren's controlling behavior and Kristy's emotionality were mutually complementary. She was encouraged to "teach" him to be more passionate, and he was urged to be her consultant on matters of organization. They grasped this way of working and though they still experienced some conflict they were able to become more affectionate with each other.

Pattern Change—Warren

A brief course of cognitive–behavior therapy for his phobic issues—with his wife as coach—worked very well. Within a short time, he found himself crossing bridges and riding escalators and elevators with relatively little or no anxiety. Similarly, a psychoeducational approach to insomnia was introduced. By modifying his evening schedule and attending to other aspects of sleep hygiene, his chronic insomnia was gradually replaced with restful sleep within 3 weeks. Efforts to modulate his constricted affect and reverse his interpersonal and empathic deficits were addressed in conjoint sessions. Thought stopping training was used in individual sessions and in prescribed homework to modulate and better control his ruminations. Finally, schema change strategies were used to modify his unrelenting/unbalanced and the emotional inhibition schemas.

Pattern Maintenance and Termination—Couple and Warren

As Kristy's dysthymia became more under her control, she experienced more satisfaction in her relationship with Warren. He was encouraged to go into business for himself, and after some hesitancy, he did. He began to work out of his home, and within 6 months his accounting practice was thriving. He gained greater control over his schedule, worked less hours and more efficiently, and found more pleasure at home. These dynamics were worked on in individual and couple therapy. After 30 conjoint sessions over a period of 14 months, the couple progressed to the point of conjoint quarterly follow-up sessions. Kristy also has individual quarterly follow-up sessions. Warren has scheduled occasional individual follow-up sessions to reflect on the level of balance in his life. Each reports considerably more satisfaction with the marriage and minimal conflict. Warren has learned to be less rigidly controlling, and Kristy, while still somewhat dramatic, feels more connected and valued.

☐ Summary

Effective treatment of obsessive-compulsive personality disorder requires that these patients become sufficiently committed to a treatment process that is tailored and focused on modifying their maladaptive obsessive-compulsive pattern. Because these patients tend to have considerable difficulty engaging in and profiting from traditional psychotherapy, an integrative-combined approach that focuses on characterological, temperament, and skill dimensions is usually essential for effective treatment outcomes. The case example illustrated the common challenges that these patients present, and the kind of clinician flexibility and competence as well as treatment resources required. It also demonstrated the process of combining individual therapy with couples therapy for the treatment of a couple in which both presented with two different personality disorders. Table 9.2 summarizes the treatment intervention strategies most likely to be effective with this disorder.

TABLE 9.2. Treatment Interventions with Obsessive Compulsive
Personality Disorder

Phase	Issue	Strategy/Tactics
Engagement	Appears eager to complete assignments	Establish collaborative contract based on patient's goal and confront resistances; Structure sessions with a problem-solving focus
Transference	Obsessive rambling; Discount clinician	Interrupt; Interpret; Redirect
Countertransference	Disengage; Isolate affect; Anger; Collude with patient's defenses	Self-monitor
Pattern Analysis	**Triggers:** Authority; Unstructured situations; Close relationships	
Pattern Change	**Treatment Goal:** "Think less, feel more"; Less perfectionistic; More spontaneous and playful	
Schema/Character	Unrelenting/unbalanced standards schema Emotional inhibition schema	Schema change strategy; Confrontation; Interpretation
Style/Temperament		
a. Affective Style	Constricted/ isolated affect	Emotional awareness training

Table 9.2 continues on page 185.

TABLE 9.2. *Continued*

Phase	Issue	Strategy/Tactics
b. Behavioral Relational Style	Procrastination; Empathic deficits; Rigidity; Interpersonal deficits	Activity scheduling; Empathy training; Interpersonal skills training
c. Cognitive Style	Ruminative; Reflective	Thought stopping training
Maintenance/ Termination	Ambivalence about termination	Wean and space out sessions

REFERENCES

Adler, A. (1956). The individual psychology of Alfred Adler. H. Ansbacher & R. Ansbacher (Eds.). New York: Harper & Row.

Alden, L. (1989). Short-term structured treatment for avoidant personality disorder. *Journal of Consulting and Clinical Psychology, 57,* 756–764.

Alden, L. (1992). Cognitive–interpersonal treatment of avoidant personality disorder. In P. Keller & S. Heyman (Eds.), *Innovations in clinical practice: A sourcebook* (vol. 2, pp. 5–2). Sarasota, FL: Professional Resources Exchange.

Allen, D. (1977). Basic treatment issues. In M. Horowitz (Ed.), *Hysterical personality* (pp. 283–328). New York: Jason Aaronson.

Allnutt, S., & Links, P. S. (1996). Diagnosing specific personality disorders and the optimal criteria. In P. S. Links (Ed.), *Clinical assessment and management of the severe personality disorders* (pp. 21–47). Washington, DC: American Psychiatric Press.

Alonso, A. (1997). The shattered mirror: Treatment of a group of narcissistic patients. *Group, 16,* 210–219.

American Psychiatric Association. (1994). Diagnostic and statistical manual of mental disorders (4th ed.). Washington, DC: Author.

Barlow, D., & Waddell, M. (1985). Agoraphobia. In D. Barlow, (Ed.), *Clinical handbook of psychological disorders: A step-by-step treatment manual* (pp. 1–68). New York: Guilford.

Beck, A. (1964). Thinking and depression: II: Theory and therapy. *Archives of General Psychiatry, 10,* 561–571.

Beck, A. (1976). *Cognitive therapy and the emotional disorders.* New York: International Universities Press.

Beck, A., Freeman, A., & Associates (1990) *Cognitive therapy of personality disorders.* New York: Guildford.

Beitman, B. (1991). Medication during psychotherapy: Case studies of the reciprocal relationship between psychotherapy process and medication use. In B. Beitman & G. Klerman (Eds.), *Integrating pharmacotherapy and psychotherapy* (pp. 21–44). Washington, DC: American Psychiatric Press.

Benjamin, L. (1993). *Interpersonal diagnosis and treatment of personality disorders.* New York: Guilford.

Bornstein, R. (1993). *The dependent personality.* New York: Guilford.

Bornstein, R. (1994). Dependency in psychotherapy: Effective therapeutic work with dependent patients. In L. Vandecreek, S. Knapp, & T. Jackson (Eds.), *Innovations in clinical practice: A sourcebook* (vol. 13, pp. 139–150). Sarasota, FL: Professional Resource Press.

Bricker, D., Young, J., & Flanagan, C. (1993). Schema–focused cognitive therapy: A comprehensive framework for characterological problems. In K. Kuehlwein & H. Rosen (Eds.), *Cognitive therapies in action. Evolving innovative practice* (pp. 88–125). San Francisco: Jossey-Bass.

Buie, D., & Adler, G. (1983). The definitive treatment of the borderline personality. *International Journal of Psychoanalytic Psychotherapy, 9,* 51–87.

Clarkin, J., & Lenzenweger, M. (Eds.). (1996). *Major theories of personality disorders.* New York: Guilford.

Cloninger, R. (1987). A systematic method for clinical description and classification of personality variants. *Archives of General Psychiatry, 44,* 573–588.

Cloninger, R., Svrakic, D., & Prybeck, T. (1993). A psychobiological model of temperament and character. *Archives of General Psychiatry, 50,* 975–990.

Coccaro, E. (1993). Psychopharmacologic studies in patients with personality disorders: Review and perspectives. *Journal of Personality Disorders, 7* (Supplement): 181–192.

Coccaro, E., & Kavoussi, R. (1991). Biological and pharmacological aspects of borderline personality disorder. *Hospital and Community Psychiatry, 42,* 1029–1033.

Costello, C. (Ed.). (1996). *Personality characteristics of the personality disordered.* New York: Wiley.

Deltito, J., & Stam, M. (1989). Psychopharmacological treatment of avoidant personality disorder. *Comprehensive Psychiatry, 30,* 498–504.

Eagle, M. (1986). The psychoanalytic and the cognitive unconscious. In R. Stern (Ed.), *Theories of the unconscious* (pp. 155–190). Hillsdale, NJ: Analytic Press.

Eckstein, D., Baruth, L., & Mahrer, D. (1992). *An introduction to life-style assessment* (3rd ed.). Dubuque, IA: Kendall-Hunt.

Ellis, A. (1979). *Reason and emotion in psychotherapy.* New York: Citadel.

Everett, S., Halperin, S., Volgy, S., & Wissler, A. (1989). *Treating the borderline family: A systematic approach.* Boston: Allyn & Bacon.

Francis, A., Clarkin, J. & Perry, S. (1984). *Differential therapeutics in psychiatry: The art and science of treatment selection.* New York: Brunner/Mazel.

Freeman, A. (1992a). Developing treatment conceptualizations in cognitive therapy. In A. Freeman & F. Datillo (Eds.), *Comprehensive casebook of cognitive therapy* (pp. 13–26). New York: Plenum.

Freeman, A. (1992b). Dysthymia. In A. Freeman & F. Datal (Eds.), *Comprehensive casebook of cognitive therapy* (pp. 129–138). New York: Plenum.

Freeman, A., & Davison, M. (1997). Short-term therapy for the long-term patient. In L. Vandecreek, S. Knapp, & T. Jackson (Eds.), *Innovations in clinical practice: A sourcebook* (vol. 15, pp. 5–24). Sarasota, FL: Professional Resource Press.

Freeman, A., & Jackson, J. (1996). Single session treatment of a borderline personality disorder. *Cognitive and Behavioral Practice, 3,* 183–208.

Glantz, K., & Goisman, R. (1990). Relaxation and merging in the treatment of the personality disorders. *American Journal of Psychotherapy, 44,* 405–413.

Glick, I., Clarkin, J., & Goldsmith, S. (1993). Combining medication with family psychotherapy. In J. Oldham, M. Riba, & A. Tasman, (Eds.), *American psychiatric press review of psychiatry* (vol. 12, pp. 585–610). Washington, DC: American Psychiatric Press.

Gunderson, J. (1989). Borderline personality disorder. In T. Karasu (Ed.), *Treatments of psychiatric disorders* (pp. 2749–2758). Washington, DC: American Psychiatric Press.

Gunderson, J., & Chu, J. (1993). Treatment implications of past trauma in borderline personality disorder. *Harvard Review of Psychiatry, 1,* 75–81.

Harbir, H. (1981). Family therapy with personality disorders. In J. Lion, (Ed.), *Personality disorders: Diagnosis and management* (2nd ed.). Baltimore: Williams & Wilkins.

Horowitz, L. (1987). Indications for group psychotherapy with borderline and narcissistic patients. *Bulletin of the Menninger Clinic, 51,* 248–318.

Horowitz, M. (1988). *Introduction to psychodynamics: A new synthesis*. New York: Basic Books.

Horowitz, M. (1995). Histrionic personality disorder. In G. Gabbard (Ed.), *Treatment of psychiatric disorders* (2nd ed., pp. 2311–2326). Washington, DC: American Psychiatric Press.

Inderbitzin, L., & James, M. (1994). Psychoanalytic psychology. In A. Stoudemire (Ed.), *Human behavior: An introduction for medical students* (2nd ed., pp. 107–142). Philadelphia: Lippincott.

Jenike, M. (1991). Obsessive compulsive disorder. In B. Beitman & G. Klerman (Eds.), *Integrating pharmacotherapy and psychotherapy* (pp. 183–210). Washington, DC: American Psychiatric Press.

Jones, S. (1987). Family therapy with borderline and narcissistic patients. *Bulletin of the Menninger Foundation, 51*, 285–295.

Kalojera, I., Jacobson, G., Hoffman, G., et al. (1998). The narcissistic couple. In J. Carson & L. Sperry (Eds.), *The disordered couple* (pp. 207–238). New York: Brunner/Mazel.

Kavoussi, R., Liu, J., & Chaucer, E. (1994). An open trial of sertraline in personality disordered patients with impulsive aggression. *Journal of Clinical Psychiatry, 55*, 137–141.

Kernberg, O. (1984). *Severe personality disorders: Psychotherapeutic strategies*. New Haven, CT: Yale University Press.

Klein, R. (1989). Diagnosis and treatment of the lower-level borderline patient. In J. Masterson & R. Klein (Eds.), *Psychotherapy of disorders of the self* (pp. 69–122). New York: Brunner/Mazel.

Koenigsberg, H. (1991). Borderline personality disorder. In B. Beitman & G. Klerman (Eds.), *Integrating pharmacotherapy and psychotherapy* (pg. 271–290). Washington, DC: American Psychiatric Press.

Koenigsberg, H. (1993). Combining psychotherapy and pharmacotherapy in the treatment of borderline patients. In J. Oldham, M. Riba, & A. Tassman (Eds.), *American psychiatric press review of psychiatry* (vol. 12, pp. 541–564). Washington, DC: American Psychiatric Press.

Lachkar, J. (1998). Narcissistic/borderline couples: A psychodynamic approach to conjoint treatment. In J. Carlson & L. Sperry (Eds.), *The disordered couple* (pp. 254–284). New York: Brunner/Mazel.

Layden, M., Newman, C., Freeman, A., & Morse, S. (1993). *Cognitive therapy of borderline personality disorder*. Boston: Allyn & Bacon.

Lazarus, A. (1981). *The practice of multimodal therapy*. New York: McGraw-Hill.

Lieberman, R., DeRisi, W., & Mueser, K. (1989). *Social skills training for psychiatric patients*. New York: Pergamon.

Liebowitz, M., Schneier, F., Hollander, E., et al. (1991). Treatment of social phobia with drugs other than benzodiazepines. *Journal of Clinical Psychiatry, 52*(11, Supplement), 10–15.

Linehan, M. (1993). *Cognitive-behavioral treatment of borderline personality disorder*. New York: Guilford.

Linehan, M., Armstrong, H., Suarez, A., et al. (1991). Cognitive-behavioral treatment of chronically parasuicidal borderline patients. *Archives of General Psychiatry, 48*, 1060–1064.

Linehan, M., Heard, H., & Armstrong, H. (1993). Naturalistic follow-up of a behavioral treatment for chronically parasuicidal borderline patients. *Archives of General Psychiatry, 50*, 971–974.

Mann, J. (1973). *Time-limited psychotherapy*. Cambridge, MA: Harvard University.

Masterson, J. (1993). *The emerging self: A developmental, self, and object relations approach to the treatment of the closet narcissistic disorder of self*. New York: Brunner/Mazel.

Masterson, J., & Klein, R. (Eds.). (1989). *Psychotherapy of the disorders of the self*. New York: Brunner/Mazel.

Meichenbaum, D. (1977). *Cognitive-behavior modification: An integrated approach*. New York: Plenum.

Miller, W., & Rollnick, S. (1991). *Motivational interviewing.* New York: Guilford.

Millon, T. (1981). *Disorders of personality: DSM-III Axis II.* New York: Wiley.

Millon, T. (1996). *Disorders of personality: DSM-IV and beyond* (2nd ed.). New York: Wiley.

Nehls, N., & Diamond, R. (1993). Developing a systems approach to caring for persons with borderline personality disorder. *Community Mental Health Journal, 29,* 161–172.

Nurse, R. (1998). The dependent/narcissistic couple. In J. Carlson & L. Sperry (Eds.), *The disordered couple* (pp. 315–332). New York: Brunner/Mazel.

Othmer, E., & Othmer, S. (1994). *The clinical interview using DSM-IV. Volume 1: Fundamentals.* Washington, DC: American Psychiatric Press.

Perry, J. (1995). Dependent personality disorder. In G. Gabbard (Ed.), *Treatment of psychiatric disorder* (2nd ed., pp. 2355–2366). Washington, DC: American Psychiatric Press.

Perry, J., Herman, J., Van der Kolk, B., et al. (1990). Psychotherapy and psychological trauma in borderline personality disorder. *Psychiatric Annals, 20,* 33–43.

Prochaska, J., & DiClementi, C. (1982). Transtheoretical therapy: Toward a more integrative model of change. *Psychotherapy, 19,* 276–288.

Reid, W. (1998). Personality disorders. In W. Reid (Ed.), *The treatment of psychiatric disorders—Revised for the DSM-III-R* (pp. 332–351). New York: Brunner/Mazel.

Salzman, L. (1980). *Treating the obsessive personality.* New York: Jason Aaronson.

Salzman, L. (1989). Compulsive personality disorder. In T. Karasu (Ed.), *Treatment of psychiatric disorder* (pp. 2771–2782). Washington, DC: American Psychiatric Press.

Schmidt, N., Joiner, T., Young, J., & Telch, M. (1995). The schema questionnaire: Investigation of psychometric properties and the hierarchical structure of a measure of maladative schemas. *Cognitive Therapy and Research, 19,* 295–321.

Shapiro, E. (1982). The holding environment and family therapy for acting out adolescents. *International Journal of Psychoanalysis, 9,* 209–226.

Siever, L., & Davis, K. (1991). A psychological perspective on the personality disorders. *American Journal of Psychiatry, 148,* 37–48.

Silk, K. (1996). Rational pharmacotherapy for patients with personality disorders. In P. Links (Ed.), *Clinical assessment and management of severe personality disorders* (pp. 109–142). Washington, DC: American Psychiatric Press.

Slap, J., & Slap-Shelton, L. (1981). *The schema in clinical psychoanalysis.* Hillsdale, NJ: Analytic Press.

Snyder, M. (1994). Couple therapy with narcissistically vulnerable clients: Using the relationship enhancement model. *The Family Journal: Counseling and Therapy for Couples and Families, 2,* 27–35.

Solomon, M. (1989). *Narcissism and intimacy: Love and marriage in an age of confusion.* New York: Norton.

Solomon, M. (1998). Treating narcissistic and borderline couples. In J. Carlson & L. Sperry (Eds.), *The disordered couple* (pp. 239–258). New York: Brunner/Mazel.

Sperry, L. (1995a). *Handbook of the diagnosis and treatment of DSM-IV personality disorders.* New York: Brunner/Mazel.

Sperry, L. (1995b). *Psychopharmacology and psychotherapy: Strategies for maximizing treatment outcomes.* New York: Brunner/Mazel.

Sperry, L., & Maniacci, M. (1998). The histrionic-obsessive couple. In J. Carlson, & L. Sperry (Eds.), *The disordered couple.* New York: Brunner/Mazel.

Sperry, L., & Mosak, H. (1996). Personality disorders. In L. Sperry & J. Carlson (Eds.), *Psychopathology and psychotherapy: From DSM-IV diagnosis to treatment* (2nd ed., pp. 279–336). Washington, DC: Accelerated Development/Taylor & Francis.

Stein, D., & Young, J. (1992). Schema approach to personality disorders. In D. Stein & J. Young (Eds.), *Cognitive science and clinical disorders* (pp. 272–288). San Diego: Academic Press.

Stone, M. (1993). *Abnormalities of personality: Within and beyond the realm of treatment*. New York: Norton.

Turner, R. (1992). Borderline personality disorder. In A. Freeman & F. Dattilio (Eds.), *Comprehensive casebook of cognitive therapy* (pp. 215–222). New York: Plenum.

Wachtel, P. (1982). *Resistance: Psychodynamics and behavioral approaches*. New York: Plenum.

Waldinger, R. (1987). Intensive psychodynamic therapy with borderline patients: An overview. *American Journal of Psychiatry, 144*, 267–274.

Waldo, M., & Harman, M. (1993). Relationship enhancement therapy with borderline personality. *Family Journal, 1*, 25–30.

Waldo, M., & Harman, M. (1998). Borderline personality disorders and relationship enhancement therapy. In J. Carlson & L. Sperry (Eds.), *The disordered couple* (pp. 285–298). New York: Brunner/Mazel.

Wells, M., Glickhauf-Hughes, C., & Buzzel, V. (1990). Treating obsessive-compulsive personalities in psychoanalytic/interpersonal group therapy. *Psychotherapy, 27*, 366–379.

Winer, J., & Pollack, G. (1989). Psychoanalysis and dynamic psychotherapy. In T. Karasu (Ed.), *Treatment of psychiatric disorders* (pp. 2639–2648). Washington, DC: American Psychiatric Press.

Woodward, B., Duckworth, K., & Guthiel, T. (1993). The pharmacotherapist-psychotherapist collaboration. In J. Oldham, M. Riba, & A. Tassman (Eds.), *American psychiatric press review of psychiatry* (vol. 12, pp. 631–649). Washington, DC: American Psychiatric Press.

Yalom, I. (1985). *The theory and practice of group psychotherapy* (3rd ed.). New York: Basic Books.

Young, J. (1994). *Cognitive therapy for personality disorders: A schema-focused approach* (rev. ed.). Sarasota, FL: Professional Resource Exchange.

INDEX